Women in Science, Engineering and Technology

and Technology

three decades of UK initiatives

Women in Science, Engineering and Technology
three decades of UK initiatives

Alison Phipps

Trentham Books

Stoke on Trent, UK and Sterling, USA

Trentham Books Limited
Westview House   22883 Quicksilver Drive
734 London Road   Sterling
Oakhill   VA 20166-2012
Stoke on Trent   USA
Staffordshire
England ST4 5NP

First published 2008

British Library Cataloguing-in-Publication Data
A catalogue record for this book is available from the British Library

ISBN: 978 1 85856 402 9

Cover credit: Reinhold Tscherwitschke. Stockphoto

Designed and typeset by Trentham Print Design Ltd, Chester and
printed in Great Britain by Hobbs the Printers Ltd, Hampshire.

Contents

GASAT members Eunice Okeke and Ina Wagner
with co-founder Jan Harding

1

Introduction

The issue of women's participation in non-traditional fields, in particular science, engineering, construction and technology (SECT), has been a long-standing concern for activists, teachers, policy-makers and those working in SECT in the UK. From the 1970s onwards and in some cases earlier, interest in the issue began to take the form of groups and projects designed to recruit girls and women to SECT fields and to facilitate their career progression. These included classroom-based action research interventions, after-school and residential courses for pupils, support and networking groups for female SECT students and professionals and training programmes for socially excluded women. However, as activity grew and developed there was little opportunity to think critically about the range of frameworks and practices or to evaluate how much progress was being made. Directories of various projects and overviews of some of the conceptual approaches being used (see for example Volman *et al*, 1995; Henwood, 1996; Vlaeminke *et al*, 1997; Faulkner, 2001; European Commission, 2003; Women Into Science and Engineering, 1988 and 2006) were not amalgamated to create a macro-analysis of theory and practice. This meant that there was little opportunity for policy-makers, educational practitioners and activists to learn from the initiatives which had been implemented.

This book is a contribution to such macro-analysis, providing an accessible history of various UK initiatives around women's participation in SECT from the 1970s to the mid-2000s. The narrative, constructed from archival and interview data, explores the aims and frameworks of around 150 initiatives, examines the practices developed and comments on what was achieved. It is always difficult to strike a balance between information and analysis, but this book will provide a useful initial reference point for educational practitioners, activists, policy-makers and scholars and will raise some interesting questions for further debate. At the time of writing, after thirty years of gender equality initiatives, girls and women continue to be under-represented in SECT fields. This points to a need to critically examine the array of attempts made to tackle the issue in order to reflect on why equality has been so difficult to achieve, to imagine how new approaches can be informed by previous successes and to chart the challenges which have been faced.

One of the key arguments of this book is that the initiatives discussed operated within limiting and often inhospitable contexts which con-strained the types of practices which could be put in place. The discus-sion in Chapter Two therefore sets the scene for the analysis, exploring various aspects of the economy, society, politics and culture between the 1970s and the mid-2000s. Economically, a key trend was the shift from a manufacturing to a service-led and knowledge economy which created a demand for women's labour in SECT fields. This ran parallel to social changes in the position of middle-class women in education and employment, occurring alongside and partly because of the emergence of the Women's Liberation Movement. This movement also inspired the development of a body of feminist literature around women in SECT, which influenced initiatives to varying degrees due to shifting attitudes towards feminism and varying levels of interaction between social science and humanities scholars and those in SECT disciplines. This feminist literature contributes usefully to the analysis presented in this book: one of the major critical points made here is that initiatives may benefit from a stronger cross-fertilisation between feminist literature, activism, policy and educational practice.

Chapter Three begins an analysis of the initiatives, with a focus on pro-jects targeted at girls' and young women's experiences of, and achieve-ments in, science and technology subjects at school. Such projects began to emerge in the early 1970s, and after a brief lull following the advent of the National Curriculum and educational restructuring in the late 1980s, were revived in the mid-1990s. The dominant approach attempted to alter girls' and young women's perceptions of science and technology in order to influence their subject and career choices. Attempts were made to create more feminine images of science and technology and to raise girls' awareness of possible career opportunities in SECT fields. Such initiatives were largely based on a deficit model of girls and young women in which their interests and understandings were problematised, a formulation which also underpinned projects developed to support women working in SECT professions, explored in Chapter Four. From the 1980s and in some cases earlier, membership organisations, informal networking groups, women's groups within professional associations and groups in universities emerged in order to help women to cope with, rather than challenge, the male-dominated structures and masculine cultures of SECT.

Chapter Five examines projects targeted at socially excluded women which aimed to empower them through the teaching of masculine skills. Women-only training courses in manual trades were an important element of the Women's Liberation Movement in the 1980s, facilitated by monies available from local authorities and the European Social Fund. From the 1990s onwards, women-only technology training also began to emerge, focused on technician and user level information and communication technologies. Both types of projects shared a common political platform and feminist pedagogic approaches focused on creating safe women-only spaces, starting from women's existing skills and experiences and empowering them to change their lives through providing them with skills, a political consciousness and emotional and financial support. This woman-centred framework differed strongly from the business case for women's participation in SECT, which came to prominence in the activist arena in the 1990s. This rhetoric focused on the benefits women could bring to SECT and the economy and became particularly influential because of skills shortages which aroused the concern of policy-makers and employers. The business case also underpinned a number of large governmental and corporate initiatives which are explored in Chapter Six.

For ease of reference, the book's four data chapters present a historical narrative followed by critical discussion in light of the relevant sociological literature. Covering thirty years of history in a single volume means that neither the factual information nor the discussion can be comprehensive: rather, the book provides evidence and an analytical framework to facilitate further debate. The examination of the various reasons for women's under-representation in SECT is not exhaustive since theory and research constituting such an analysis already abounds in the broad body of literature. The statistics give an impression of the position of women in SECT at different points in time but do not constitute a longitudinal statistical analysis of women's under-representation. This book fills a gap in the literature by analysing attempts made to tackle the problem of gender inequality in SECT. Some of the archival sources used in this book are currently housed at the UK Resource Centre for Women in SET in Bradford: this has been noted in the bibliography. The limitations of the sources must be acknowledged: although many requests for information were circulated and a large number of groups and individuals contributed materials and memories, it is likely that a substantial number of initiatives were overlooked because no records or people were available. And the initiatives included can be only briefly described, which does not do them full justice.

The initiatives researched were largely based in England because of the greater availability of data but projects based in Wales, Scotland and Northern Ireland are included where possible. Due to constraints on space, projects from countries outside the UK are featured only if they were launched in or had a substantial collection of participants from the UK. Similarly, web-based organisations are included only if they demonstrated a large UK user base. General gender equality initiatives have not been incorporated unless they were particularly relevant to girls' and women's participation in SECT, and SECT initiatives targeted at both sexes have largely been excluded, although it is more than likely that such initiatives had beneficial effects. Projects set up before the 1970s have only been covered if they continued into the period which is the focus of the book, although initiatives around women in SECT clearly have a longer history. The acronym SECT has been used to refer to science, engineering, construction and technology, even though some groups have focused only on science, engineering and technology (SET) and some school-based initiatives only on science and technology.

Countless individuals and institutions have been involved in the pre-paration of this book, and while it would be impossible to list them all, I would like to acknowledge those who provided resources, information and support. Financial backing was provided by Sussex University and the European Social Fund through an EQUAL partnership managed by the UK Resource Centre for Women in SET (UKRC), which commis-sioned the research. The Economic and Social Research Council and Cambridge University funded earlier research which has contributed significantly to this volume. The team at Trentham Books, and in parti-cular Gillian Klein, have been positive and helpful throughout the process and I am delighted to be added to their list of authors. I am also very grateful to Maggi Ray-Jones for her eagle eyes and excellent sugges-tions made at the proofing stage. The book was suggested and inspired by Jan Harding, an indefatigable activist for women in SECT whose per-sonal archive provided an invaluable resource. Additional material came from the archive of the late Joan Mason, another tireless and inspirational activist. Numerous other individuals provided materials and memories, including Jane Butcher, Ruth Carter, Ann Clarke, Laura Davies, Sara Delamont, Judy Ekins, Sylvia Gibbs, Caroline Gregory, Clem Herman, Melody Hermon, Karen Hindersley, Pat Langford, Lisa Mairah, Jeanette McMurdo, Terry Marsh, Rosa Michaelson, Karen Procter, Marion Scott, Ailsa Swarbrick, Peter Templeton, Rachel Tobbell, Pam Wain, Claire Welburn, Liz Whitelegg, Ros Wollen, Nicky Wrigley and the staff at the Women's Library.

In exploring this enormous volume of information, I was lucky to have the capable research assistance of Kathrine Jensen, Rochelle Mondesir, and Leigh Ingham. Project management support was provided by Annette Williams and Anna Zalevski of the UKRC, both of whom were obliging and encouraging throughout. Other staff at the UKRC also helped to gather information and publicise the research. The writing process was overseen by a steering group consisting of Annette Williams, Anna Zalevski, Jane Butcher, Clem Herman, Liz Whitelegg, and Gill Kirkup: their input came at a crucial stage and significantly shaped my thinking. In the course of my analysis I also drew on con-versations with a number of colleagues and past supervisors including Madeleine Arnot, Diane Reay, Flis Henwood, Harriet Marshall, Heather Mendick and Katrina Miller. A number of people provided intellectual and emotional support, including friends and colleagues Lesley McMillan, Paula Black, Gill Bendelow, Susie Scott, Julien Morton and Charlie Masquelier, friends Laura Riley and Becky Donoher, my parents Jan and Mike and my brother Simon. Thomas Wallner deserves thanks for being my more talented partner in the extra-curricular musical activities which help me to stay sane in academia. I am grateful to Gabby Barker for coordinating Gender Studies at Sussex so efficiently that I managed to find time and space to write. Last but not least, thanks to my students for keeping me on my toes and keeping my energy levels high.

Finally, I would like to pay tribute to the outstanding women and men who have worked towards gender equality in SECT with so much energy and commitment. As I gathered and processed the information presented here I was increasingly impressed, not only by the number of individuals who have been involved but also by the dedication which has been shown, which in many cases has constituted a lifetime journey. It has been a privilege to meet, talk to and in some instances get to know so many bright and extraordinary people. I realise that the narrative I have composed only goes a small way towards representing their efforts and achievements and that there are inevitably errors and omissions. It is impossible to reproduce history exhaustively or entirely accurately, but I hope that this account will be accepted as a partial yet helpful analysis of an important period of activity around women's participation in SECT, and that the critical points made here are taken in the supportive and constructive spirit in which they are intended.

2
A changing context

This chapter sets the scene for the book, exploring some of the relevant economic, political, social and cultural trends that characterised the period between the 1970s and the early 2000s. First, it examines economic shifts which created a demand for women's labour in SECT fields to maintain the UK's position in an increasingly competitive globalised marketplace. Secondly, it describes social changes in the position of women which encompassed growing success for the professional middle classes alongside deepening inequalities between women in terms of class and ethnic background, all of which occurred in the context of a privatising and marketising welfare state. Thirdly, it discusses the emergence of the women's liberation movement in Britain, which contributed to improvements in women's social position and provided the impetus and umbrella for some of the initiatives discussed in this book. It concludes with an examination of the body of feminist literature around gender and SECT, which was linked to the wider canon of feminist theory and which also informed a number of initiatives. The information presented in this chapter is not comprehensive, since it would be difficult to cover the history of this period even in an entire book. The chapter is a rough contextual framework, not a definitive historical narrative.

1. Gender, capitalism, and globalisation: three decades of economic change

In the domestic context the relative prosperity of the immediate post-war period ended in the 1970s. Unemployment remained above 3 per cent for most of the decade and had reached 4.7 per cent by 1979 (Pope,

1998, p60). Oil prices quadrupled in 1973 due to the formation of the OPEC (Organisation of Petroleum Exporting Countries) cartel, a sharp shock to a British industry which was dependent largely on foreign fuel. Partly as a result, traditional manufacturing industries such as textiles, iron and steel began to decline. In addition, inflation stood at 20 per cent or more and there was a sterling crisis in late 1976 which forced the government to seek a loan from the International Monetary Fund (Pope, 1998, p53). During the Winter of Discontent of 1978 to 1979 there was a wave of strikes throughout the public sector over pay. All these developments contributed to a massive swing towards the Conservatives in the 1979 General Election and 'the most marked shift of opinion since 1945', as the country moved to the right (Sked and Cook, 1993, p323).

The 1980s thus began with an economic slump. Thatcher's government put a raft of microeconomic measures in place under the banner of efficiency, such as tax reform, privatisation and restriction of trade union power, and eased credit regulations to facilitate an expansion in consumer spending (Pope, 1998, pp64-66). Following this, a period of economic growth sustained itself for the rest of the decade. However, this failed to eliminate the problem of unemployment due to the decline in manufacturing and the labour economies which were being made even in prosperous industries as part of the practice of downsizing (Seldon and Collings, 2000, p66). By 1989 the economy was in the midst of another downturn: growth had slowed, exports had failed to keep pace with the mounting imports that were feeding the consumer boom and unemployment and inflation were again on the rise (Pope, 1998, p66).

Much like the 1980s, the 1990s saw a slump at the beginning of the decade. However, although this economic downturn was more dramatic than that of the 80s, by 1993 it was over and Britain was growing at a faster rate than most of her economic rivals (Pope, 1998, p66). This was partly due to the rapid growth of the high-tech and service sectors, and although the trend of downsizing continued, demand for skills in these areas meant that unemployment had fallen to 5 per cent by the end of 1997 (Pope, 1998, pp67-68). By the late 1990s key indicators such as growth and employment were relatively healthy (Eatwell, 2003, p173). In 2002 the UK was placed sixth of the 25 European Union

Member States in terms of its Gross Domestic Product (GDP) (Equal Opportunities Commission, 2002; p2), and by 2004 unemployment was lower than at any time since the late 1970s (Equal Opportunities Commission, 2000, p5).

The process of globalisation supplied the broad context for these economic trends, encompassing the development of increasingly global markets for products, the expansion and diversification of consumer demand and the rise of mass technological information transfer, communication, and travel (Young, 1998; Castells, 2000; Magalhâes and Stoer, 2003). Across the West, there was a shift from Fordist economies centred on material production towards knowledge markets for symbolic commodities such as technologies and services (Seldon and Collings, 2000; Skills and Enterprise Network, 2001). As part of this process, the so-called neoliberal principles of rule by market forces, privatisation, competition and individualism began to reign supreme in Western states and to be exported to the global South via trade under the guise of economic and social progress. This international trading structure was reliant on the societal division of labour in which Western economies focused on capital-intensive, high value-adding production and peripheral societies in the South were reduced to performing labour-intensive, low value-adding production tasks (Waters, 2001).

Within the hyper-competitive globalised economic structure Western governments and corporations became increasingly preoccupied with maintaining their status. For corporations this meant strategic alliances with other firms, migration of production processes to offshore plants in the developing world, where labour was cheaper and laws less stringent, and processes of upskilling and downsizing whereby an ever-shrinking domestic labour force was expected to perform a greater variety of tasks (Magalhâes and Stoer, 2003). For governments this included making efforts to reform national infrastructures in the service of the free market and to ensure the supply of sufficient and appropriately trained human capital (Strathdee, 2005). The globalised worker was expected to possess high levels of technical knowledge (Waters, 2001), soft skills such as strategic and project management, teamwork and communication (Mason, 1999; Mitter, 1995) and the facility to work flexibly and to undergo a process of continuous professional development (Magalhâes and Stoer, 2003).

Science, engineering, and technology were key sectors in globalising Western economies due to the close relationship between technological progress, innovation and economic growth. Scientific and technical firms in the UK began to report and predict skills shortages in the 1990s and early 2000s because of increased human capital requirements linked to globalisation. In 2000 over two-thirds of UK employers with 25 or more employees reported skills shortages driven by the emergence of new technologies, changing work practices and increased competition (Department for Education and Employment, 2000; Millar and Jaggar, 2001). In 2002 the Roberts Review identified problems in the supply of science, engineering, and technology skills, citing increasing demand for professionals in these fields alongside declining numbers of graduates (Roberts, 2002). The shortage of qualified professionals in the emergent and growing information technology, electronics and communications (ITEC) sector was seen as a serious handicap to the European economy and accounts of a growing ITEC skills crisis in Europe in the early 2000s reported an estimated shortfall of 860,000 workers (Millar and Jaggar, 2001).

In the context of these skills shortages the UK government began to pay increased attention to women's under-representation in scientific and technical fields and to view their labour as a panacea for economic ills. In 1993 the Office of Science and Technology White Paper *Realising Our Potential* positioned women as the country's single most under-used economic resource. Following this, *The Rising Tide*, a commissioned report by the Committee on Women in Science, Engineering, and Technology, made a case for attracting and retaining women in these fields to 'improve the UK industrial position in increasingly competitive world markets' (Committee on Women in Science, Engineering, and Technology, 1994, p1). In 2002 the report *SET Fair*, submitted by Baroness Susan Greenfield to the Office of Science and Technology, argued that the under-representation of women in science, engineering and technology threatened, 'above all, [the UK's] global competitiveness' (Greenfield *et al*, 2002, p9). The report's rationale for equality in SET was rooted in the concepts of productivity, innovation, and Britain's competitive position in the world economy (Greenfield *et al*, 2002, p27).

2. Equality but not for all: social and political change and gender relations

By the time the UK economy became dependent on their labour, white middle-class women had made huge strides in education and the workforce, although women from working-class and ethnic minority backgrounds faced deepening disadvantage. The creation of the welfare state in the aftermath of the Second World War contributed to a shift in gender relations through providing universal and free secondary education and generating new employment opportunities for women in welfare-related professions (Arnot *et al*, 1999), and by 1971 47 per cent of married women were economically active (Lewis, 2003, p161). There were changes in family patterns in the 1970s which included a dramatic increase in the divorce rate, a continuation of the increase in illegitimate children which had started in the 1960s, a rise in one-parent families and a concomitant high incidence of female and child poverty. However, what appeared to be a position of increased freedom and choice for many women actually brought new forms of regulation of their material and emotional lives, through doctors in the case of contraception and abortion and counsellors in the case of divorce (Lewis, 1992, p5).

Despite the deteriorating economy of the 1970s the Labour government put a raft of left wing social policies in place, including intensified comprehensivisation of schools, deceleration in the sale of council houses, and phasing out private practice from the NHS (Sked and Cook, 1993, p293, 300). A number of emergent social and political movements, including the women's movement, drew on the ideas of meritocracy and equality of opportunity which had characterised the post-war social democratic consensus and which were still in the political mainstream at this time. Partly due to feminist pressure the 1970 Equal Pay and 1975 Sex Discrimination Acts were passed, as well as the 1975 Employment Protection Act which established statutory maternity rights. By the late 1970s women's issues were on the agenda of trades unions, local councils, and the Labour Party (Segal, 1987). Nevertheless, official support of women's issues may have been more apparent than real (Bassnett, 1986, pp161-162), and legislation only tackled inequalities at the most basic levels. For instance, the provisions of the Equal Pay Act were of limited use in a labour market characterised by escalating horizontal segregation which meant that women's jobs were by nature the lowest paid (Segal, 1987).

The Conservative General Election victory of 1979 ushered in a Thatcherite ideology based on very different principles: individualism, consumerism, and competition. For the so-called New Right inequality was a necessary condition of modern societies (Arnot *et al*, 1999) and the post-war commitment to equality of opportunity an attempt at social engineering which disrupted this natural order. During the 1980s the government implemented cutbacks to the welfare state through the privatisation of various social services and providing inducements for people to opt out of state provision by buying their council houses and sending their children to private schools with government help (Seldon and Collings, 2000, p71). Market systems and values were introduced into the public sector, perpetuating competition between hospitals, social service departments and schools, while state control was concurrently increased through policies such as the introduction of a national curriculum (Seldon and Collings, 2000).

The Thatcherite policy package was underpinned by the belief that allowing individuals to compete freely within market structures would enable them to succeed regardless of their gender, ethnicity or class background, as long as equal access was guaranteed and a framework of legislation was in place to prevent overt discrimination (Wilkinson, 1999, pp29-30). Although prosperity increased during this period, the policy of leaving society to the invisible hand of the market actually enhanced social differentiation and inequality since market structures relied on the creation of winners and losers (Arnot *et al*, 1999; Seldon and Collings, 2000; Cook and Martin, 2005, p2). During the 1980s the number of people dependent on income support and one-parent benefits increased from 3.4 million to over 5.5 million and the proportion of families with no full-time wage earner rose from 27 to 37 per cent. In 1979, the richest 10 per cent of the population owned 20.6 per cent of the nation's wealth while the poorest 10 per cent owned 4.3 per cent: by 1991 these figures had shifted to 26.1 and 2.9 per cent respectively (Seldon and Collings, 2000, p78).

The undisputed social winners during the period of Conservative government were white middle-class professionals and service workers in the knowledge economy and women were prominent in this group.

The labour market feminised rapidly during this time as many traditional men's jobs in manufacturing became obsolete (Wilkinson, 1999; Julius, 2000). During the 1980s it became generally accepted that even women with children were justified in going to work (Pugh, 2000) and by the mid-1980s state benefits for married women no longer assumed a male breadwinner (Segal, 1987). However, the pay gap between the sexes remained substantial, partly because economic recession had entrenched many women in low-paid and insecure jobs (Segal, 1987, p42) and the glass ceiling remained almost impenetrable (Pugh, 2000). In addition Thatcher tried to restore Victorian values and domestic ideologies to society during her period of office, but failed because of the changed social landscape, the impact of the women's movement and her own commitment to the free market which demanded women's labour (Arnot *et al*, 1999; Wilkinson, 1999).

By 1991 the labour market included 59 per cent of married women, although often in low-status and low-paid jobs and often also working part time. Women's employment was largely in caring professions, many of which were within the welfare state: some feminists saw this as a new form of patriarchy in which women undertook caring jobs in the public sphere which reflected those they performed at home (Lewis, 2003, p264). Women's increasing participation in the labour market on more equal terms with men was not matched by an increase in the participation of men in domestic tasks (Vogler, 2005). There had been a further shift in family structures: by 1997 married people were 54 per cent of the adult population of England and Wales as against over two-thirds in 1971; the divorced, who had been one per cent of the adult population in 1971, now accounted for 7 per cent (Equal Opportunities Commission, 2000). In 1997 37 per cent of births occurred outside marriage, as compared with 6 per cent in 1961 (Equal Opportunities Commission, 2000).

During the 1990s John Major's Conservative government continued to push the Thatcherite social policy agenda and in many social services business representatives replaced those from Local Authorities and direct government grants and private funding supplanted local monies. The Private Finance Initiative was introduced in 1992, forcing Local Authorities to contract out the management and delivery of social services to the private sector (Farnsworth, 2006, p819). Despite the re-masculinisation of curriculum and pedagogy which had resulted from the 1988 Education Reform Act (Arnot and Miles, 2005, p174) and partly as a result of the introduction of a National Curriculum which to some extent standardised educational trajectories, girls' performance in many subjects began to surpass that of boys (Arnot *et al*, 1999). As a result of this a moral panic began to materialise in policy and public opinion around the issue of boys' underachievement (Francis, 1999; Skelton, 1998). However, this obscured the far greater widening since the 1980s of inequalities based on social class and ethnicity (Gilborn and Mirza, 2000).

After the 1997 New Labour landslide the government continued the privatisation and marketisation of the public sector, along with intensified business participation in social policy and welfare services, for instance through Health Action Zones and Foundation Hospitals with private sponsorship (Shaw, 2003; Farnsworth, 2006, p825). The Private Finance Initiative was expanded under Public Private Partnerships to build and in some cases manage schools, roads, and hospitals (Farnsworth, 2006, p827). New Labour's Third Way ideology was an attempt to transcend neoliberalism and old-style social democracy and incorporated a shift in the conceptualisation of the welfare state from the provision of economic security to an investment in human capital (Pascall and Lewis, 2004, pp374-5; Genz, 2006, p334; Meredith, 2006). This meant that training was a key concern and the involvement of business in education was solidified through Education Action Zones, Specialist Schools, and City Academies. Learning and Skills Councils replaced the Training and Enterprise Councils, with the aim of providing a better fit between education and national and local skills needs (Farnsworth, 2006, p824).

Because of the gains made by the women's movement and increased demand for their labour, by the early 2000s women made up almost half the labour force and it was projected that by 2011 57 per cent of women aged 16 and over would be economically active (Equal Opportunities Commission, 2000). Girls continued to outstrip boys at school: in 2004 58 per cent of girls (as opposed to 47 per cent of boys) in the UK gained five or more A* – C grades at GCSE or equivalent (Equal Opportunities Commission, 2004). However, despite this progress 44 per cent of women in employment (as opposed to 10 per cent of men) worked part time, and women working full time earned 82 per cent of what men earned per hour (Equal Opportunities Commission, 2004). Growing social and political individualism and the continued conceptualisation of family life as an essentially private matter meant that efforts to promote women's participation in the labour market were not combined with support for their caring responsibilities (Pascall and Lewis, 2004, pp377-8).

Also, despite the gains made in education and in the workforce, women were still under-represented in traditionally masculine fields, even after more than thirty years of initiatives and despite the renewed official interest in women's contribution to the science and technology base. Between the mid-1990s and the early 2000s women's representation among first degree students in scientific and technological fields had largely increased, but in engineering and technology it remained low at 17 per cent, and in computer science it was 22.4 per cent. At postgraduate level the proportion of female students in all fields had increased but women were 23.1 per cent of engineering and technology students and their representation in computer science had dropped to 28.3 per cent in 2002/03 after a high of 29.2 in 2000/01 (UK Resource Centre for Women in SET 2007). Outside the academy, women's training followed similar patterns: modern apprentices in hairdressing and early years care and education were mainly women, while those in construction, engineering and plumbing were mainly men (Equal Opportunities Commission, 2004).

By 2004 women were 44.5 per cent of workers in all occupations and the majority of workers in administrative and secretarial (80%) and personal service jobs (84%) (Equal Opportunities Commission, 2004). However, they represented only 4.7 per cent of engineering professionals, 1.4 per cent of workers in the skilled metal and electrical trades, and 0.8 per cent of workers in the skilled construction and building trades (UK Resource Centre for Women in SET, 2007). Social class and ethnic divisions between women had widened, particularly between increasingly successful white, middle-class professionals and the working-class and ethnic minority women who performed low-level service jobs or took on middle-class women's caring responsibilities (Arnot and Miles, 2005; Acker, 2004). Despite 30 years of social and political change and dramatic progress for some groups of women, by the mid-2000s substantial inequalities remained.

3. The drive for women's liberation: (re)birthing a political movement

A large proportion of the progress made in terms of gender relations between the 1970s and the 2000s can be attributed to the emergence of the second wave women's liberation movement in Britain (Arnot and Weiner, 1999). Some time after the birth of second wave feminism as a set of ideas in both Europe and the US, the first National Women's Liberation conference, held at Ruskin College Oxford in 1970, cemented the foundations of British activism. The increased politicisation of women within student politics and the growing New Left and an increasing militancy over the issue of equal pay among women in the labour movement were two of the major catalysts for the emergence of a movement which brought together pre-existing women's groups and created new forms of activism. There was no single unifying ideology (Bruley, 1999), but initial demands were concerned mainly with formal legal equality: equal pay, equal education and job opportunities, free contraception, abortion on demand, and free 24 hour nurseries. Subsequent demands included legal and financial independence, an end to discrimination against lesbians and the right for women to define their own sexuality and freedom from violence or sexual coercion. Overall, the movement envisaged an end to the laws, assumptions and institutions that perpetuated male dominance and aggression (Segal, 1987).

The movement drew on the insights and polemics of early second wave feminist writers such as Simone de Beauvoir, Germaine Greer, Juliet Mitchell, Shulamith Firestone and Kate Millett, although its everyday tactics owed more to women's experiences in grassroots peace and labour politics. Socialist and Marxist feminisms were more influential than liberal feminism in Britain at this time but movement practices drew heavily on liberal strategies, encompassing debates, conferences, publications, and marches which were designed to raise public awareness and influence politicians (Pugh, 2000). The biggest demonstration of the 1970s occurred in 1976 when 100,000 participants protested against proposed restrictions to the provisions of the Abortion Act of 1967 (Nash, 2002, p325). However, the movement was also characterised by a disillusionment with mainstream politics and legal processes, an idea of the state as essentially patriarchal and a desire to avoid its masculine structures: the alternative to this was small, non-hierarchical women's groups within which a variety of activities were undertaken (Nash, 2002, p316, 319).

Grassroots movement initiatives during the 1970s included drop-in centres for self-education, alternative health practices, nurseries, rape crisis provision and domestic violence refuges (Nash, 2002, p319). Many incorporated a strong focus on consciousness-raising or women sharing their experiences of sexism, under the banner of 'the personal is political'. Many feminists created non-traditional models of femininity, which were ridiculed in the media (Bassnett 1986, p156) and which later figured prominently in the anti-feminist backlash (Toller, Suter and Trautman, 2004). There was no overarching organisational body but publications such as *Women's Report* (founded in 1971) and *Spare Rib* (founded in 1972) provided some collation of what was going on.

At the same time, Women's Studies began to develop as an academic subject focused on uncovering and reclaiming women's history, studying feminist theory and women's literature and engaging with alternative perspectives on women's health. Juliet Mitchell's course at the Anti-University in London in the summer of 1969 was the first Women's Studies course, after which others developed, many organised by the women's centres which were emerging in towns and cities. In the late 1970s and 1980s universities began to develop Women's Studies curricula, some delivered in mainstream modules and courses and some taught by activists within the community (Bird, 2002, p140). As the women's movement moved into the academy there was conflict over whether it belonged there or whether it was primarily characterised by activism, although many Women's Studies faculty and students attempted to combine both aspects through on-campus activities (Bird, 2002).

By the end of the 1970s and in the context of a general political shift to the right, divisions were becoming apparent within the movement. The majority of feminists were dissatisfied by the Equal Pay and Sex Discrimination Acts of 1975, although it was generally thought that these laws had satisfied women's demands: the declining Labour government was now using this popular belief to ignore further calls for change (Pugh, 2000). As a result the movement shifted its energies towards the issue of sexual politics, and to stress the call for liberation rather than equality. There had always been tension in the movement between the two concepts: equality which consisted of admission to traditionally male-dominated areas and practices and liberation which encouraged women to live according to their own values and priorities (Whelehan, 2000, p13). From the late 1970s onwards liberation took centre stage although the idea that economic independence would bring liberation remained an important theme.

Although the women's movement was a major source of opposition to the Thatcher government of the 1980s, it lacked a central organisation and focus (Segal, 1987). This was partly due to increasing fragmentation: fierce confrontations occurred at the final national conference in 1978 and black feminists, lesbian feminists and working-class feminists argued that their voices were not being heard and took opposing political platforms. There was a parallel external battle: the New Right assault on social justice movements plus a growing anti-feminist backlash in society meant that during the 1980s and into the 1990s feminists were scapegoated for social and moral decline (Whelehan, 2000). In the context of economic shifts which meant that many traditionally male jobs were becoming obsolete, an increase in the male suicide rate and a drop in boys' educational performance, theories began to emerge about the women's movement having gone too far (Faludi, 1992; Callaghan *et al*, 1999; Hawkesworth, 1999).

As the movement shifted away from simple equality politics, and in an attempt to create a sense of sisterhood in the midst of fragmentation and attack (Segal, 1987), the 1980s saw the intensification of feminist theorising and practice based on the idea of difference. Difference feminists purported that men inevitably wielded oppressive power over women because of their inherent aggressiveness and competitiveness and that women's qualities of nurturance and care were a superior basis on which to take society forward. This was seen most prominently in the theory of eco-feminism and the activist practices of the women's peace movement: significantly the women's peace camp on Greenham Common. The first group of women arrived in 1981 after the government's decision to locate 96 cruise missiles at the RAF Greenham airbase: the protest rapidly grew and incorporated non-violent direct action to blockade and disrupt nuclear convoys. During the 19 years the camp was active it housed women from many parts of the UK and elsewhere, some of whom were arrested, as well as convoys of visitors (Hipperson, 2006).

During the 1980s many women's centres, health groups and other women's organisations had been forced to shut down due to a lack of funding. In the 1990s the women's movement changed form in the context of a continued backlash against feminism, a decline in participation in traditional politics and a rise in participation in single issue organisations. So-called third wave groups began to emerge, many focused on particular themes including violence against women, sweatshop exploitation, reproductive freedom, race and class, queer issues, workforce and career issues, and welfare rights (Nash, 2002, p312; Jacob and Licona, 2005, p201). Although this new generation adopted many second wave feminist practices, they rejected second wavers' perceived harshness towards femininity and dominant white middle class viewpoints. Instead, third wavers sought a diverse range of perspectives and political positions, some of which had been controversial in the past such as those which were pro-pornography and anti-abortion (Jacob and Licona, 2005, pp198-199). In response, some second wavers characterised third wavers as ungrateful, ambivalent and lacking in political focus (Jacob and Licona, 2005, pp199-200; Nash, 2002).

In the realm of formal politics New Labour, in moving away from its conventional trade union base, made new alliances including mobilising prominent party women in the 1990s (Bashevkin, 2000). The party introduced women-only shortlists for winnable seats in 1990 and set up a Women's Unit after winning the 1997 General Election (Nash, 2002, p313). Five women were appointed to the 1997 Blair cabinet, including the publicly identified feminist Harriet Harman (Bashevkin, 2000, pp407-8). During the 1990s femocrats, or civil servants identified with the issues if not the politics of the women's movement, became increasingly powerful in mainstream political institutions (Chappell, 2002). Many second wave issues became mainstream, such as domestic violence, childcare, masculine work cultures and sexual harassment (Nash, 2002, p313). However, New Labour distanced itself from the feminist label even though women were promoted to political office, and its Third Way ideology was based on social exclusion rather than inequality, with an individualist ethic which did not resonate with second wave feminism's commitment to collective action (Genz, 2006). There was little substantial policy change during the party's first term in office (Bashevkin, 2000).

During the 1990s and early 2000s there was a growth in the production and distribution of feminist ideas across academia (Nash, 2002, p313). Some Women's Studies practices such as starting from students' experience, learning by doing, and facilitating interactive discussions, had become orthodox within the pedagogy of adult education (Bird, 2002, p147). However, in an academic context in which the deconstructivist currents of postmodern, poststructural and queer theories were becoming stronger (Nash, 2002, p314), many Women's Studies departments within universities were re-profiled as Gender Studies departments, which broadened their theoretical remit but threatened their political connections. Cuts in university funding and the trend towards quantitative and policy-focused social research also meant that many Women's and Gender Studies departments were shut down. Within the women's movement there were splits between those within the academy and those without, with academics being constructed as careerist, bourgeois, elitist, obtuse, greedy and overly rationalistic at the expense of the emotional world (Bird, 2002, p147). By the early 2000s the women's movement looked increasingly conflicted and fragmented, although it had made impressive gains since the 1970s.

4. Women in science, engineering, and technology: the how and the why

A body of feminist literature around women's participation in science, engineering, construction and technology (SECT) built up in tandem with the women's movement from the early 1970s. The earliest theme was women's under-representation in SECT education and work, reflecting the concerns of both first and second wave liberal feminisms with middle-class women's education and employment more generally and growing as science and technology became more central to the economy (Wacjman, 2004, p13; Rose, 1994, p12). Early studies examined horizontal and vertical gender segregation within SECT fields, and documented barriers such as girls' socialisation, sex stereo-typing, a lack of role models, the masculine image of science and technology and the impact of women's caring responsibilities (Wacjman, 2004, p14; Rose, 1994, p14; Rosser, 2005, p2; Henwood, 2000, p210; Fox Keller, 1992, p42). Suggested remedies included equal opportunities policies and compensatory socialisation processes which put the onus on girls and women to change and positioned SECT as essentially neutral and positive (Faulkner, 2001, p79; Henwood, 2000, p210; Wacjman, 2004, p14).

Studies of the reasons for women's under-representation in SECT were produced at the same time as analyses of the consequences of this inequality in terms of the selection of scientific problems, the design of experiments and the interpretation of data, especially in the human sciences (Fox Keller, 1985). Feminist empiricists mounted challenges to the selection and definition of scientific problems and the design and interpretation of research, in particular the then common practice of making generalised claims on the basis of all male animal or human samples (Harding, 1986, pp22-23; Harding, 1992, p59; Tuana, 1992, p101). Working from a conception of science itself as essentially neutral, these feminists argued that such sexism and androcentrism were a question of bias and could be corrected by a rigorous application of scientific method. They contended that women were likely to be superior scientists because of the probability that they would be more vigilant about such bias (Harding, 1986, pp24-25; Tuana, 1992, pp100-101). Feminist empiricists therefore claimed that improving the representation of women in science was necessary to correct scientific knowledge but were criticised for being apolitical and supporting a masculine definition of objectivity by other feminists who had begun to see science itself as a masculine project (Fox Keller, 1985, p177; Tuana, 1992, p102).

Alongside liberal feminist efforts to improve the representation of women in SECT professions, socialist, radical, and eco-feminists mounted a critique of SECT cultures, epistemologies and practices in the 1970s and 80s (Fox Keller, 1985; Rose, 1994, p2). Harding (1986, p9) characterises this as a shift from the 'woman question in science' to the 'science question in feminism', and Rose (1994, p12) argues that these currents of thought were particularly dominant in the British women's movement because of the strong radical and socialist feminist strands within it. These feminists examined the links between SECT and masculinity, identifying men's dominance in science and technology as an important source of their power in a capitalist society. Some feminists explored the impact of technologies on women's lives, in studies which ranged from optimistic analyses of the creation of new and more interesting jobs to pessimistic anxieties about machines taking over women's roles and threatening their health and safety (Wajcman, 2004, p24). In the context of the theorisation of housework as a key site of women's oppression (Oakley, 1974), socialist feminists argued that the sexual division of labour prevented women from controlling technology either at work or at home, and pointed out that the mechanisation of the home had not reduced the amount of time women spent on domestic tasks (Wajcman, 2004, p27-28).

Cynthia Cockburn's (1983; 1985) analyses of the historical development of various trades and technologies in the context of shifting social structures highlighted how the development of industrial capitalism interacted with changing forms of patriarchy to enhance men's power over women through their power over technology. It was argued that women had been historically and systematically excluded in various ways from the techniques and languages of technical practice (Benston, 1992, p34). Cockburn's theorisation of the mutually shaping relationship between masculinity and various technologies was an important foundation for the feminist science and technology studies which later developed (Faulkner, 2001).

At the essentialist end of the spectrum eco-feminists highlighted the intertwining of technology with masculine agendas and especially with institutions such as militarism and the globalising corporation (Benston, 1992, p35). They claimed that modern science and technology were inextricably implicated in practices of domination and death, the corollary to which was a view of women as nurturers, pacifists and humanists (Rose, 1994, p2-3; Wajcman, 2004; Benston, 1992, p36). These socialist, radical and eco-feminist interpretations were technologically determinist in the sense that they viewed technology as inescapably bound up with masculinity and saw little or no possibility of agency or change. They were underpinned by a conceptualisation of women as powerless victims of patriarchal science and technology (Wacjman, 2004, p23). Feminists working in craft fields and promoting women's participation in the manual trades, however, saw a source of empowerment for women in the acquisition of technical skills (Wajc-man, 2004, p12).

The women's health movement which emerged in the 1970s was an important impetus for future feminist analyses of the gendered meanings embedded in scientific knowledge. This movement incorporated a two-fold focus: the suppression of women's knowledge and healing skills and the way in which health sciences and technologies oppressed women through defining and controlling their bodies (Wajcman, 2004, p17). Feminists in the field of health developed practices to facilitate women's understanding of their own bodies in resistance to the dictates of the scientific establishment, exemplified in the book *Our Bodies Our-selves* (Rose, 1994, p72). Feminist biologists began opposing science's construction of women's natures (Rose, 1994, p20, 71). Studies such as *Alice Through the Microscope* and *Women Look At Biology Looking At Women* (Fox Keller, 1985, p45) documented the uses and abuses of biology and fed into debates about how science had been used in the service of sexist, racist, classist and homophobic ends (Harding, 1986, pp21-22). These interventions ran parallel to a general societal and academic resurgence of biological determinism, epitomised in the debates raging around IQ, which were challenged by some black feminists (Rose, 1994, p19).

Within philosophy and the sub-discipline of philosophy of science feminists were deconstructing and questioning Western knowledge structures and arguing that modern science was constituted around a set of gendered conceptual dualisms (Fox Keller, 1992, p47). The seminal 1983 text *Discovering Reality*, edited by Sandra Harding and Merrill Hintikka, contained articles by authors such as Ruth Hubbard, Evelyn Fox Keller, Jane Flax, and Nancy Hartsock (Harding and Hintikka, 1983, pix-xix), whose work positioned established frames of thought as inadequate tools for understanding the realities of women's lives (Harding and Hintikka, 1983, pix, x). This book was an early example of the practice of reading science as a text to discover the hidden social meanings embedded within it (Harding, 1986, p23). The authors drew on the disciplines of philosophy, literary criticism, history and psychoanalysis to deconstruct science as being grounded in masculine perspectives on masculine experience and to identify aspects of women's experience which could provide a basis for knowledge (Harding and Hintikka, 1983, px).

By the mid-1980s a critique of the masculine project of reason and objectivity, its applications (particularly in terms of militarism) and its construction of women as incompatible with rational and scientific thought was maturing. Feminists in different disciplines grappled with the question of whether the problem was male dominance of science and technology or whether there was an inherent masculinity and patriarchy embedded in scientific knowledge and practice (Wajcman, 2004, p12). This fed into attempts to develop alternative epistemologies and questions about the possibility of a feminist science (Wajcman, 2004, p18; Fox Keller, 1985; Rose, 1994, p23). There were also efforts to reclaim the history of women as scientific practitioners, particularly in Women's Studies courses which focused on retrieving women as historical figures. In 1983 Evelyn Fox Keller combined the two themes in her biography of Barbara McClintock, exploring the scientific practice McClintock developed which was driven by a 'feeling for the organism', or intimate attention and patient observation (Fox Keller, 1985, p49; Rose, 1994, p16-17).

Influenced by Marxist ideas around the privileged epistemological position of subordinated groups, feminist standpoint theorists such as Dorothy Smith, Nancy Hartsock and Patricia Hill Collins argued that women in general, and feminists in particular, were able to produce a qualitatively different and superior scientific knowledge (Harding, 1992, p60; Rose, 1994, p95). Their analysis focused on women's reproductive and caring activities and the gaps between dominant conceptual schemas and women's experiences (Harding, 1992, p61; Rose, 1994, p76-77). It was argued that feminism and the women's movement could develop women's ways of knowing into an epistemology (Harding, 1986, p26). Such theories were later criticised by feminist postmodernists who asked how a standpoint could possibly be attributed to women, whose experiences were so evidently divided by class, race, and culture. Theorists such as Donna Haraway argued that epistemological perspectives should embrace such fractured identities as fruitful grounds for enquiry and focus on localised and specific knowledges rather than overarching truths which were inseparable from the exercise of power (Harding, 1986, pp26-28; Rose, 1994, p23).

Wajcman (2004) argues that dualisms and black and white thinking plagued much of the feminist analysis of gender and SECT conducted from the 1970s onwards. Many studies positioned both gender and SECT as pre-given categories or 'black boxes', rather than deconstructing the ways in which each informed the other (Henwood and Miller, 2001). In the 1980s however, some feminists began to draw on Dinnerstein and Chodorow's feminist object relations theory which theorised the interaction of the social with the biological and conceptualised masculinity and science as mutually constitutive. Emotional and intellectual development was viewed as progressing from early symbiotic closeness with the primary care giver to gradual separation and individualisation, a process which was thought to occur differently in girls and boys (Rose, 1994, p74-75). It was argued that because the primary care giver was generally female, the development of a masculine identity and self-concept demanded separation from the feminine world of feelings and desires, and this propelled some boys and men towards the emotionless rationality of science (Fox Keller, 1985, p11, 70).

By the 1990s this mutually reinforcing interaction between masculinity and science was being theorised within the developing field of feminist science and technology studies (STS). This emergent discipline was influenced by sociology, history, and philosophy and drew elements from the radical science movement of the 1960s (Rose, 1994, p21). Studies focused on the simultaneous construction of men, women, and so-called technoscience and saw all as socially shaped (Fox Keller, 1992, p47). Mainstream STS, which had emerged since the 1970s, had developed a sociological analysis of the content and direction of innovation and had positioned technological change as contingent on social contexts (Wajcman, 2004, p33, 37). Feminists applied a gender lens to this idea of a reciprocal traffic between technoscience and society, and examined how gendered meanings interacted with technoscience in terms of both design and usage (Wajcman, 2004, p38). In such studies neither gender nor technoscience existed prior to one another or prior to the social process.

Feminist STS provided a framework within which to deconstruct the political and cultural underpinnings of technoscience. Donna Haraway's work on primatology showed how it was created within and thus shaped by particular contexts and power relations and how it was informed by gendered and racist assumptions (Rose, 1994, p85-91). Her work was part of wider deconstructivist developments in feminist theory as a result of the postmodern and poststructural turn (Rose, 1994, p21). Ideas around gender and performance, prominently elucidated in Judith Butler's work, fed into the emergent area of cyberfeminism and its exploration of the potential of the Internet to be a tool for liberation and the cyborg an agent in alternate realities (Rosser, 2005, p17). The idea of the performativity of gender, combined with the idea that technoscience was socially shaped, opened up spaces for examining possibilities of women transforming technoscience through different types of social relations and gendered performances (Wacjman, 2004, p54).

Conclusion

Between the 1970s and the 2000s a variety of economic, social, political and cultural trends came together to provide the context for initiatives around women's participation in SECT. Economically, the growing demand for women's labour in scientific and technical fields which accompanied globalisation created a rationale and policy impetus for gender equality initiatives. Increasing numbers of middle class women became available as a human resource as social changes facilitated their participation in the labour market. The shift in gender relations was partly due to the emergence of the women's liberation movement, which provided a strong voice for equality and an umbrella for activism and initiatives. Feminist scholars had begun to analyse and deconstruct science and technology, although such theories had little impact on practice. Groups, networks, and projects focused on women's participation in SECT appeared. This book examines some of these initiatives, comments on their underlying principles and practices, and attempts to understand their achievements and limitations and the challenges they faced in working towards gender equality.

3

The problem with girls
Educational projects from the 1970s to the 2000s

This chapter focuses on the activity targeted at girls and young women in education which aimed to improve their achievements in science and technology subjects and arouse their interest in related careers. The initiatives took place in two major phases: an initial phase which emerged in the early 1970s and a resurgence which occurred alongside a renewed policy interest in women's participation in SECT in the mid-1990s. Projects took various forms, including grassroots curriculum interventions and action research conducted by teachers and academics, workshops and events organised by LEAs, universities and colleges, short courses and awareness raising campaigns developed with government or corporate support and broad national and international initiatives such as Women into Science and Engineering (WISE) and the Gender and Science and Technology (GASAT) Association. The dominant approach employed in these initiatives was a compensatory model, focused on counteracting sex-role socialisation through changing the image of scientific and technical subjects and raising the awareness of girls and young women about opportunities in these fields. This chapter examines a number of the initiatives, highlighting some of the limitations of the dominant model while noting the challenges posed by the UK education system as a context for activism and grassroots educational activity.

1. Setting the scene: gender and school science and technology

Although women's access to paid work and the professions was a key theme for both first and early second wave feminist movements, a field of initiatives around the issue of women's education in SECT did not coalesce until the mid 1970s. The construction of girls and women as a reserve of unrealised talent by government and industry, along with the expansion of second wave feminist activism, acted as catalysts for the appearance of this first phase of projects. The 1975 Sex Discrimination Act was a major catalyst since it provided a framework within which sexism and sex differentiation in education could be highlighted and discussed as a policy issue, while the newly formed Equal Opportunities Commission amassed a body of statistical evidence of gender inequality (Arnot *et al*, 1999, p71). As a result, feminists in teaching and academia were able to dovetail demands for equal opportunities with concerns about the lack of skilled labour in SECT professions. Girls' relative underachievement in scientific and technical subjects at secondary school and the channelling of girls and boys into separate areas of the curriculum were positioned in terms of their potential labour market implications and social justice (Arnot *et al*, 1999).

Girls and women were well represented in the biological sciences at the time, but were a minority in the physical sciences. A 1973 Department of Education and Science survey of a sample of 10 per cent of state-

Table 3.1 O-level option choices in a sample of maintained schools, 1973

		Being offered (% of total)	Taking (% of total)
Physics	Boys	90	47
	Girls	71	12
Chemistry	Boys	79	27
	Girls	76	17
Biology	Boys	88	28
	Girls	95	49

(Department of Education and Science 1975, p11)

maintained schools in England demonstrated the gendering of option choices for O-level examinations and revealed that some girls were not even being offered the traditionally masculine subjects (see Table 3.1).

In 1976 four times as many boys as girls were entered for O-level physics, and five times as many boys as girls were entered at A-level nationwide. Twice as many boys as girls were entered for both O- and A-level chemistry. However, in biology almost twice as many girls as boys were entered for O-level and the ratio at A-level was roughly even (Walford, 1980, pp220-221). Girls' under-representation in the physical sciences at school impacted on the university degrees they were eligible for: in 1979 only 5 per cent of engineering students at universities were women (Engineering Industry Training Board, 1987, p8) and in 1981 women were only 9.4 per cent of students entering university engineering and technology courses (National Electronics Council, undated, p2). The number of women enrolling on degree courses in computer science was declining, from 22.4 per cent of total applicants in 1979 to 10.9 per cent in 1986 (Women into Computing, 1988).

From the mid 1970s, teachers, academics and policy-makers began to produce a growing body of literature about this problem. Much of this drew on liberal feminist ideas, identifying barriers to equal opportunities such as socialisation processes and gender stereotypes which steered girls away from scientific and technical subjects and the masculine image of SECT. The key factor was choice: girls were thought to be opting out of SECT subjects because of conflicts between their gender socialisation and the masculine image of these fields and because they lacked role models to inspire them to challenge gender stereotypes. Suggestions for encouraging girls and young women to choose SECT focused mainly on changing their perceptions and attitudes. Schools and teachers were advised to raise girls' and parents' awareness of SECT careers through distributing literature and multimedia materials and holding events and workshops. It was also suggested that older pupils, university students and practicing SECT professionals could act as role models. SECT curricula were re-written in order to include examples which were related to girls' interests or more radically repositioned in contexts such as social issues and the human body. Teachers were encouraged to prevent boys from dominating discussions and commanding too much attention. Pedagogic approaches which included hands-on experimentation were also put forward, often as a means to avoid the abstractions which were thought to be off-putting to girls. At school level suggestions were made about restructuring the option choices made at ages 13-14 for O-levels if these were based on obviously gendered clusters of subjects.

The 1970s and 1980s also saw the emergence of more critical and radical feminisms within education which conceptualised schooling as a key institution of patriarchy infused with male values and knowledge which discriminated against female students and staff (Arnot *et al*, 1999, p76; Weiner, 1994, p79). These frameworks focused on the power relations, social structures and masculine cultures within which girls' and women's educational and career choices were made (Henwood, 1998). The channelling of girls away from SECT was seen as a means of excluding them from an important source of power in a capitalist society and a manifestation of gendered discourses which constructed women as unable to exercise scientific rationality and technical skill (Marshall, 1997). The feminist pedagogies which were based on these interpretations of schooling centred on the notion of empowerment and the value of perceived feminine qualities such as nurturance and care. Teachers were encouraged to examine classroom power relations, and the idea of single-sex schooling was often put forward as a means for helping girls and young women to find their voices away from masculine domination. Activists and teachers working within these frameworks concentrated on localised consciousness-raising activities, critically engaging with school cultures and attempting to reshape subjects such as history or English to include women's experiences and achievements (Arnot *et al*, 1999, pp74-75).

Although such critical and radical feminisms undoubtedly informed the development of activity around girls and SECT, liberal feminism was the dominant strand of thought in the formulation of educational initiatives and government publications launched at this time generally drew on received liberal feminist wisdom. The Department for Education and Science report *Girls and Science*, published in 1978, listed a number of factors which were thought to be influential in girls' rejection of mathematics and science subjects. The report concluded that the most powerful factors were early socialisation and the home environment, societal stereotypes and the gender stratification of the employment market, although the science curriculum was also thought to play a part. The Cockcroft Report (Cockcroft, 1982) highlighted a need for appropriate careers guidance and for teachers to be aware of the differences in mathematical performance between boys and girls. The Physics Education Committee of the Royal Society and the Institute of Physics reported in 1982 that many girls had unfavourable attitudes towards science which were caused by social, psychological and cognitive factors such as the masculine and impersonal image of science, girls' perceptions of their own femininity and their interactions with and the expectations of parents, teachers and peers. It also argued that the attitudes and practices of teachers, the presentation of the curriculum and the structuring of option choices were key (Physics Education Committee, 1982, p1).

2. The first phase of initiatives

a. Grassroots interventions

The emergence of girls' and young women's under-representation and under achievement in SECT education as a problem for policy-makers, teachers and activists gave rise to the first phase of educational activity designed to supplement the existing curriculum and influence girls' educational choices. Many of these projects took place at grassroots level, consisting of small-scale curriculum interventions or action re-search investigations conducted by teachers, sometimes in partnership with interested academics. The devolved curriculum and organisation of schooling before the Conservative Education Reform Act of 1988 meant that these teachers enjoyed a degree of autonomy in their every-day practices and were able to institute bottom-up reforms (Weiner, 1994; Arnot *et al*, 1999). But this did not mean that school environments were flexible and amenable to change, and often the strategies developed most successfully were those that could be carried out without too much disruption to normal schooling practices (Weiner, 1994, p77). Some of the grassroots activities that were carried out are described below: many more individuals and schools were also developing small-scale projects, but information on them is difficult to obtain.

In 1979 the Association for Science Education set up its Girls and Physical Sciences (GAPS) Sub-Committee under the leadership of Jan

Harding (Taber, 1991, p222). Its main task was to collect examples of school-based initiatives and to publish them in the ASE bulletin *Education in Science*. The first such article detailed an initiative set up by Michael Hearn, a science teacher at a mixed comprehensive school in Essex, Bedfords Park. Hearn's strategy for encouraging girls to opt for the physical sciences incorporated various forms of awareness raising such as discussing the issue with pupils in the third form (age 13-14) classes, giving parents guidance at parents' evenings and briefing the school Careers Officer. Hearn also sought to raise awareness among teachers who were involved in the options process. Evening events were held in science laboratories, and a poster campaign was developed. Hearn reported that the intervention was successful in raising interest in the physical sciences, although mostly among high-achieving girls (Hearn, 1979).

In 1982 the science staff at Ellis Guilford School, a mixed comprehensive in Nottingham, developed a variety of strategies to increase the number of girls studying physical sciences. This initiative blended liberal-feminist awareness raising approaches with more critical and radical themes such as curriculum redesign and single-sex teaching. The input of careers advice to third year pupils was increased in a bid to alert them to the importance of their option choices to future career opportunities. Girls only groups were instituted in physics and chemistry for the upper ability band of the school's third year and teachers tried to modify their interactions with pupils in mixed-sex classes to prevent the boys dominating. The science syllabus was re-designed to present science concepts through students' experience. The initiative resulted in more girls opting for physics and chemistry and fewer girls opting for biology. It had a wider impact too, inspiring the development of the GEMSAT project in Nottingham (Price and Talbot, 1984).

Mary Doherty, Head of Science at Westwood High School for Girls in Croydon, launched an initiative in 1983 to generate interest in the physical sciences. Doherty altered the presentation of the physics curriculum to stress the relevance of science to social and environmental issues and introduced regular pupil assessments in the hope that charting girls' progress would increase their confidence. She advised science teachers to prevent boys from commandeering most of their attention, to avoid making or tolerating comments which supported gender stereotypes and to be vigilant about boys' attitudes to girls in general. Awareness raising strategies were put in place such as augmented careers advice, talks to parents, and visits from working women scientists and engineers who acted as role models. In 1987 Doherty reported that although many of her female school leavers planned to go into fields such as banking, hairdressing and beauty therapy, some had decided to pursue science at A-level or to aim for non-traditional careers (Doherty, 1987).

As part of PhD research conducted between 1983 and 1987, teacher Judith Ramsden implemented a small-scale action research initiative at her secondary school which was focused on stimulating third form girls' interest in physics and encouraging them to pursue the subject further. This involved designing two new course units which contrasted with the existing traditional textbook-based curriculum. This new curriculum material built on the interests of both genders, presented physical science concepts through pupils' everyday experiences and the human body, and stressed the social and applied aspects of science. The two units were initially taught by Ramsden, who used innovative approaches such as problem solving, creative writing, role play and discussion. She reported that pupils responded favourably, with a majority ranking the units as those they had most enjoyed. The numbers of both boys and girls selecting physics in their option choices increased (Ramsden, 1990).

Jan Harding's pioneering 'Chemistry from Issues' course, delivered to fourth and fifth form (age 14-16) pupils during the early 1980s at Chelsea College, exemplifies a project led by an individual teacher which had significant impact. It is also an early example of a context-based or humanistic approach to teaching science to girls. Rather than making use of examples related to girls' interests, Harding's course involved a wholesale recontexualisation of the chemistry curriculum using various social and environmental issues connected to the use of chemical materials, such as the decline of the British steel industry, animal testing of cosmetics, and global warming. This approach was both radical and innovative in its use of social issues as the purpose and context for scientific investigation. As a result of her work, Harding was asked to contribute to the Salters Chemistry courses in the 1980s which proved popular with female students (personal communication). However, the introduction of the National Curriculum in 1988 instituted a traditional approach to science teaching nationwide and reduced teachers' flexibility to implement such radical initiatives (Murphy and Whitelegg, 2006, p18). Harding was also central to the GATE project at Chelsea College and the founding of the Girls and Science and Technology (GASAT) Association, which became the Gender and Science and Technology Association and was ongoing in the mid-2000s.

As well as projects carried out by individual teachers, the first phase generated a number of projects focused on teacher networking and support. GAMMA (the Girls and Mathematics Association) was a grassroots collective of academics focused on supporting teachers' activity and disseminating good practice around gender and mathematics (Arnot *et al*, 1999). Valerie Walkerdine and Rosie Warden, researchers at the Institute of Education's Gender and Mathematics Unit, founded the association in 1981. GAMMA operated mainly through monthly meetings of its London collective, although there was also an active group in Leeds and Bradford and an annual conference held in various locations including Goldsmiths, King's College, and South Bank University. A number of further education colleges and teachers centres also became associated with the collective. It is difficult to determine whether the association's activities had a direct impact on girls' and young women's educational and career choices but GAMMA members were able to influence mainstream mathematics education significantly in later years either as National Curriculum developers or schools mathematics inspectors. After the group went into decline in the late 1990s some members went on to support initiatives such as the International Organisation for Women in Maths Education and European Women in Mathematics, and these were ongoing in the 2000s.

Women into Computing (WiC) was founded in 1984 during a meeting of academics at Edinburgh University at which a sudden fall in female applicants to computing degrees was discussed. The collective subsequently encouraged young women into computing through building bridges with industry and schools and organising workshops for schoolgirls and conferences for teachers. The organisation eventually grew to incorporate academics, teaching staff and students in universities, polytechnics and colleges of further education (Women into IT,

1990b). In 1987, the collective CWEST (Cornwall Women in Engineering, Science and Technology) was formed by a group of female scientists and engineers at the University of Exeter. CWEST's activities in schools included lectures, careers awareness workshops and hands-on experimentation with girls in small groups. These were initially targeted at third year girls in the process of choosing their options for O-level and GCSE, but the collective subsequently broadened their focus to cover pre-A-level and A-level students who were considering courses at university.

b. Formalised projects

Alongside these small-scale curriculum interventions many teachers and academics were involved in larger and more formalised projects, often operating with governmental or corporate support. These projects were a supplement to existing teaching and as such employed models focused largely on awareness raising and altering the presentation of SECT curricula. The Girls and Science Education project, conducted by Jan Harding and Jan Craig between 1974 and 1975, involved a detailed statistical investigation of 1974 O-level science results to publicise factors which influenced the achievement of girls (Harding and Craig, 1978). The Girls and Technology Education (GATE) Project followed in 1981 to 1984, managed by Harding and Gay Randall and supported by British Petroleum (BP). GATE investigated ways of improving the curriculum and assessment of craft, design and technology (CDT) subjects at secondary level, making use of context-based approaches. The project aimed to encourage competence in design and technology amongst girls and to increase interest in the mathematical and physical sciences. Harding and Randall engaged in in-depth classroom observation, produced guides for parents and curriculum materials for teachers and oversaw experimentation with single-sex teaching groups (Harding and Randall, 1983; Weiner, 1994).

This model of curricular reform and teacher support informed many of the formalised initiatives developed during the first phase, many of which had official support in the form of sponsorship from Local Education Authorities (LEAs). The Tameside Girls and Science initiative, launched in 1981 and supported by the Tameside Metropolitan Borough Council, involved science teachers Janet Dawe and Gill

Rhydderch spending half their week working with science teachers in other schools, helping them to develop girls' interest and achievements in the sciences. Dawe and Rhydderch worked to raise girls' awareness of the social aspects and implications of science, and to keep school science departments informed of developments in research and teaching. Short courses were run in which girls were able to engage in hands-on experimentation (Dawe and Rhydderch, 1983). Work was also undertaken with careers advisers and girls about to choose their O-level options (Morton and Price, 1984, p7).

The GEMSAT (Girls' Education in Mathematics, Science and Technology) project was carried out in Nottinghamshire between 1984 and 1985. Supported by the Nottinghamshire LEA, Sandra Morton and Jean Price worked with teachers in eight secondary schools. They focused on altering the presentation of curricula in line with girls' interests, supporting teachers in attempting to put gender-equitable practices in place, developing links between schools and local industry and making girls aware of the opportunities available in mathematics, science, and technology. As part of its awareness raising the project aimed to show girls that achievement in mathematics, science, and technology was 'a normal, accepted part of feminine behaviour' (Morton and Price, 1984, p5). Initiatives varied between schools but included using videos and posters to promote science to girls, modifying science corners to make them more attractive to girls and experimenting with single-sex teaching. Many of the schools also received a visit from the WISE Bus, a mobile technology classroom.

In 1983 the London Borough of Croydon produced a set of guidelines for good practice in the teaching of IT for the Equal Opportunities Commission. The Girls and Information Technology Project was set up, sponsored jointly by the EOC and Croydon LEA. It focused on awareness raising, information gathering and evaluation: the project worker visited secondary schools to raise awareness around girls and IT, evaluate the effectiveness of existing teaching materials and the EOC guidelines, identify good practice, establish links with local industry, and make contact with parents. The final project report recommended that teachers should examine their literature and displays to check for gender stereotypes, develop more inclusive teaching styles, avoid specialist jargon, ensure that girls could access adequate support, consider implementing single-sex teaching, examine the structuring of option choices and put more effort into careers education (Equal Opportunities Commission, 1985). Between 1985 and 1986 the EOC partnered the Sheffield LEA on a similar project. Project worker Judith Ellis helped five primary schools to develop equal opportunities guidelines and provided information and support around using computers as teaching tools (Ellis, 1986).

In the early 1980s and with the support of the EOC, the Young Women's Christian Association (YWCA) was involved in a research programme which examined young women's processes of adjustment to working in traditionally male fields. GETWISE programmes developed from this research: residential courses for young women encompassing outdoor hands-on activities, role modelling and awareness raising. The courses were offered twice a year in London and were linked to companies such as Ford, Marconi and British Gas. In the late 1980s concern about the needs of young women in rural areas led the YWCA to develop a similar course in manual trades which was piloted in Devon. This course was funded by the Rural Development Commission, the Equal Opportunities Commission, British Gas and Devon General (YWCA of Great Britain, 1991).

During the 1980s the Youth Training Scheme (YTS) was the main route into the construction industry for young people. This national scheme was funded and managed by the Manpower Services Commission, with 60 per cent of the construction courses delivered by the Construction Industry Training Board (CITB). At this time the proportion of young women on construction YTS courses was less than 2 per cent, as a result of which the CITB appointed an equal opportunities officer in 1988 (Eclipse Publications, 1990, p18). This led to the introduction of an equal opportunities policy and a national plan of action, implemented on a regional basis. In Greater London and the South East, ten girls' schools were targeted for outreach work, although these initiatives met with resistance from teachers and the girls themselves (Eclipse Publications, 1990, p19). At national level the MSC ran a competition for YTS trainees to produce a poster or write an essay on equal opportunities and held a Young Women in YTS conference. To gain approved status from the Commission at this time YTS training organisations had to demonstrate that they were making efforts in the area of equal opportunities, and a number of dedicated single-sex schemes were set up (Manpower Services Commission, 1988).

In 1982 Prime Minister Margaret Thatcher officially launched the Manpower Services Commission's Technical and Vocational Education Initiative (TVEI), which aimed to support schools and colleges in developing full-time four year vocational courses for students between the ages of 14 and 18 (Dale *et al*, 1990, p22; Lee, 1996, p3). The overall objective was economic rather than educational, driven by the new vocationalism of the 1970s and 80s which directly linked vocational education and training to industrial productivity and economic growth (Dale *et al*, 1990, p22; Yeomans, 1996, pp4-5). TVEI was launched shortly after the passage of the Sex Discrimination Act which made gender equality a prominent objective (Lee, 1996, p13, 43). Progress was initially limited, as many TVEI projects failed to address equal opportunities fully and some may have promoted gender segregation by offering packages with either secretarial or technology and science emphases (Dale *et al*, 1990, pp144-145). However, in later phases and partly due to pressure from the Manpower Services Commission (Dale *et al*, 1990, p145), the equal opportunities agenda became more embedded. Strategies put in place included making traditionally gendered subjects compulsory for both sexes, altering curricula and teaching styles, linking traditional option choices to non-traditional ones, single-sex teaching, re-labelling subjects in gender neutral language, organising non-traditional work experience programmes and taster courses, and delivering dedicated equal opportunities modules (Dale *et al*, 1990, pp148-150; Lee, 1996, pp44-45).

As TVEI progressed, it became evident that girls were not taking up opportunities to engage in non-traditional training, and that in fact there had been a decline in their participation in science and craft, design and technology (CDT) within the project (Dale *et al*, 1990, p141). There were also clear sex differentiations in work experience, with boys choosing manufacturing, craft and technical placements while girls worked in offices, travel agents, and personal service businesses such as hairdressers and caterers (Her Majesty's Inspectorate, 1991, p19). By the end of TVEI there had been a redefinition of the interpretation of equal opportunities within the project, with a focus on equalities generally rather than gender issues in particular and an attempt to revalue traditionally feminine areas of the curriculum and labour market in the face of fruitless attempts to recruit girls to so-called masculine areas (Dale *et al*, 1990, p142). After the National Curriculum was introduced in 1988 TVEI became increasingly marginalised and ended in 1997 (Yeomans, 1996, p2, 4). In terms of gender equality the initiative had a lasting impact because of its insertion of equal opportunities into mainstream educational discourse (Dale *et al*, 1990, p137). The project also cemented the ideological links between schooling and the economy, to the extent that subsequently it became difficult not to refer to the instrumental purposes of education (Dale *et al*, 1990, p4). This new vocationalism undoubtedly influenced many of the projects described in this chapter.

One day workshops and short residential courses were run at colleges and universities during the first phase, which were designed to introduce girls to scientific and technical concepts through lectures and hands-on experimentation and to raise their awareness of career opportunities in SECT. Many of the courses were run with the support of local industry and used undergraduate and postgraduate students, academics and industry professionals as role models. The target group was mainly fifth and lower sixth form girls who were already studying sciences or mathematics, in a bid to encourage them to choose SECT subjects in further or higher education. Institutions running such courses in the 1970s and 80s included the universities of Bradford, Essex, Glasgow, Liverpool and Sussex, polytechnics in Manchester, Sheffield City and the South Bank, the Dundee College of Technology, and the North East Wales Institute of Higher Education (WISE, 1988; Women into Computing, 1988; Women Into IT, 1990a). Some academics also worked with younger girls: during the 1980s the Polytechnic of North London ran a project entitled the Selective Programme in Science and Engineering (SPISE) in which third form girls undertook evening activities with undergraduates and lecturers and which reportedly encouraged a high uptake of O-level physics by girls (Taber, 1991, p224).

During this time many LEAs became publicly committed to equal opportunities in education. One of the first such commitments was made by the Inner London Education Authority (ILEA), which set up its Standing Committee on Career Opportunities for Women and Girls in

1970 and officially adopted an Equal Opportunities policy in 1981 (Morrell, 2000). LEA activity which focused on girls and SECT during the 1970s and 80s included research around option choices and exam results, courses for teachers and workshops for pupils, links established with grassroots and formalised projects, experiments with single-sex teaching and careers guidance. LEAs engaged in such activity included Brent, Ealing, Doncaster, Walsall, Avon, East Sussex, Isle of Wight, Sheffield, and Croydon (Madden, 2000). By 1987 an EOC survey of LEAs to ascertain to what extent they were implementing gender equality policies found that 50 per cent were taking some form of action (Madden, 2000, p43-44). Central government initiatives carried out during the first phase of activity included the Schools Council Project Reducing Sex Differentiation in Schools, which between 1981 and 1983 developed and disseminated good teaching practice. The Secondary School Curriculum Review was set up in 1982, supported by the Department for Education and Science and the Association for Science Education and included a commitment to redress girls' disadvantages in science education (Arnot *et al*, 1999).

Between 1985 and 1987 a number of Local Education Authorities, universities, polytechnics and colleges hosted Women's Training Roadshows funded by the Department of Trade and Industry, various national employers, and the Manpower Services Commission (Women's National Commission, 1987, p3). These two or three day events were designed to provide information and raise awareness of opportunities in non-traditional areas of education and work (Women's National Commission, 1987, p2). Activities included showing videos and putting on plays, workshops, exhibitions, interaction with role models and distributing booklets (Women's National Commission, 1987, pp4-6). Over 20,000 schoolgirls and hundreds of women visited the roadshows and the Women's National Commission reported positive reactions but recognised that the model would need to be replicated on a larger scale to have a lasting impact (Women's National Commission, 1987, p6). Evaluation of the Cardiff Women's Training Roadshow in 1987 revealed that although a majority of the 500 schoolgirl participants enjoyed the experience and felt they had been informed about non-traditional careers, most remained interested in stereotypically feminine jobs (Pilcher *et al*, 1989).

1984 was designated as Women into Science and Engineering (WISE) year. The WISE Campaign was set up, and WISE year provided a banner for numerous grassroots and formalised initiatives throughout the UK, many conducted on a one-off basis. Four primary schools, eleven secondary schools, seven LEAs and 61 universities were involved in putting on lectures and exhibitions, hands-on workshops and short courses, careers conventions, school visits by women scientists and seminars and conferences for parents and teachers. Many initiatives were run or supported by NGOs, government bodies and corporations such as the North London Science Centre, the Institution of Mechanical Engineers, British Aerospace, Esso, IBM, the Association for Science Education, the Women's Engineering Society, the EOC, Westland Helicopters, and British Gas (Equal Opportunities Commission, 1985). The Fawcett Library WISE exhibition was also opened in 1984, financed by the Inner London Education Authority. It was targeted primarily at schoolgirls and aimed to raise awareness about the achievements of women scientists past and present. The scientists featured included Jocelyn Bell Burnell who discovered pulsars, pioneer of computer programming Grace Hopper, geneticist Rosalind Franklin and the first woman professor of physics in England, Daphne Jackson. In subsequent years the exhibition toured libraries and schools throughout the country (Walton, 1984).

Case Study 3.1: Girls Into Science and Technology
Girls Into Science and Technology (GIST) was set up in 1979 by Alison Kelly, a lecturer at Manchester University and Judith Whyte, a lecturer at Manchester Polytechnic. This longitudinal action research project aimed to help teachers to reduce girls' underachievement in science and to encourage more girls to consider careers in SECT fields (GIST, 1979). As well as the partnership between academics and teachers incorporated in the project, there was also input from government and industry: the Social Science Research Council, the EOC, the Department of Industry Unit, the Schools Council, and Shell UK Ltd provided funding (GIST, 1979; GIST, 1984). GIST's approach focused on the role played by schools in sex-role socialisation, which reflected the received wisdom of the time and saw the school as the site where it would be easiest to create change. The researchers worked with teachers at eight co-educational comprehensive schools in Manchester and a further

two schools were used as controls (GIST, 1984, p2). The sample was the pupil cohort starting secondary school in September 1980 who were followed until the point at which they chose their O-level options in the summer term of 1983 (GIST, 1979, p14).

Project interventions focused on making the school context more girl-friendly and on altering the perceptions and attitudes of girls. GIST researchers undertook classroom observations and ran workshops in the selected schools to educate teachers about sex-role socialisation and its relationship to girls' underachievement in science and technology (GIST, 1979, p10). Attempts were also made to alter teaching practice: interventions included single-sex teaching, work experience for girls, the use of senior girls as role models, de-stereotyping curriculum materials and encouraging pupils' awareness of gender issues in the classroom (GIST, 1984, pp15-18). The project team also devised the VISTA Scheme (Women Scientists and Technologists Visit Schools) to counter stereotypes by providing role models for girls and non-traditional examples for boys (Whyte, 1985, p45). They organised careers roadshows for pupils and two conferences to enable teachers to network and share ideas around good practice (GIST, 1984, pp9-13).

Evaluation of the project revealed some success in changing attitudes. Both girls and boys participating in the project became less stereotypical in their attitudes to jobs, more enthusiastic about entering non-traditional fields and more positive about science (GIST, 1984, pp24-25). The girls were more likely than those from the control schools to aspire to a job with some scientific or technical element, more likely to say they wanted to be employed if they had young children and less likely to say they wanted their future husband to be cleverer than themselves (GIST, 1984, p28). However, these attitudinal shifts were not reflected in pupils' option choices, except in the case of a small number of mainly middle-class girls (GIST, 1984, p19; Kelly, 1988). A postal questionnaire distributed to the cohort a year after they reached the statutory school leaving age of sixteen indicated that some girls were planning careers with a scientific or technical element and were progressive in their general attitudes around gender. However, this questionnaire was only returned by 58 per cent of the cohort, and these were disproportionately the most academically successful and advantaged (Kelly, 1988, p78). The GIST project had an impact on teacher attitudes around gender, but the researchers found that changing the schools was more difficult and largely depended on their existing ethos (GIST, 1984, p34; Kelly, 1988, p81).

The GIST researchers concluded that the impact of the project had been limited because schools do not operate in isolation: parents, peers and employers also played a role in girls' under-achievement in science (GIST, 1984, pp39-40). In later work Alison Kelly acknowledged that the GIST perspective had been too heavily focused on the internal states of girls and had conceptualised the image of science as masculine when in fact the nature of science was masculine (Kelly, 1987, p2). The project problematised girls and the contexts in which they were educated rather than engaging critically with the broader social context and the cultures and knowledge structures of science. Attempts to change the attitudes of pupils and teachers were not accompanied by an analysis of where those attitudes came from and the power relations they reflected and perpetuated. This reflected the liberal-feminist thinking of the time, which conceptualised science and technology as neutral and challenged gender stereotypes but did not ask questions about how and why they came into existence. However, GIST's longitudinal model and practices of partnership between academic researchers and teachers could have facilitated an analysis of the underlying causes of inequality, unlike the supplementary, short-term, government and corporate driven projects which dominated the second phase of activity from the mid-1990s onwards.

Case Study 3.2: Engineering Industry Training Board Initiatives
The Engineering Industry Training Board (EITB) developed a number of initiatives from the late 1970s which included scholarships to facilitate girls' study of technical subjects and short courses to stimulate their interest in engineering careers. The overarching theme was the perceived image problem of engineering: the EITB aimed to persuade girls and their teachers, parents, and careers advisers that engineering was an appropriate career choice, and to 'dispel the popular misconception' that engineers were all 'boiler-suited maintenance [men]' (Engineering Industry Training Board, 1987, p1). The first project to be put in place was the Technician Scholarship Scheme which ran between 1976 and 1978 in Birmingham and London and allocated fifty scholarships to

female school leavers for a two year girls only technical training course. On completing the course the girls were helped to find job placements in which to finish their training. Although there were problems recruiting the first cohort because of head teachers' hostility and because few girls had the required O-level physics, a total of 142 girls participated in the scheme, 58 of whom completed the training process. But it was not clear whether any of them eventually found work (Engineering Industry Training Board, 1987, pp3-4).

Due to discomfort around the perceived artificiality of the single-sex training environment, the fully job-based Girl Technician Grant Scheme replaced the Technician Scholarship Scheme in 1979. This was designed to encourage employers to train more young women on the job by providing grants for the trainees. The scheme ran until 1985. Over 800 girls were recruited, with about 100 employers taking part each year. The majority of employers reported that the trainees were successful and managed to find suitable careers: the three most common areas of employment were quality assurance, draughting, and design and development. Questionnaires sent to the first two years' cohorts revealed that over half the young women felt that they had received more help during the training process because they were female. Some reported that colleagues reacted better to them and they were able to have less confrontational relationships than the men (Engineering Industry Training Board, 1987, pp5-7). But over half had problems with the attitudes of male colleagues and instructors, and because the scheme was not longitudinally evaluated it was not clear whether these attitudes mitigated against the female trainees progressing in their fields.

EITB short courses were also launched in 1979, starting with the Insight programme. This programme was designed to encourage able sixth form girls to consider careers in engineering professions through spending a week in residence at a university or polytechnic learning about higher education and career opportunities in engineering. The aim was to 'dispel the popular misconceptions that engineering is mainly manual work, physically demanding and carried out in a noisy and dirty environment' (Engineering Industry Training Board, 1987, p8). Practising women engineers were allocated as leaders to small groups of girls to act as role models and provide first-hand information about careers in engineering. One full day was spent at an engineering firm. The first course was developed by Geoff Chivers at Loughborough University and demand was so great that in subsequent years courses were run at nine or ten universities, catering for about 400 girls each year. Between 1981 and 1985 the programme was evaluated and achieved relative success in terms of the number of female participants who were considering studying engineering at university or who had applied to an engineering course (Engineering Industry Training Board, 1987, pp8-12). Unlike other first phase initiatives, the Insight programme was sustained into the 2000s.

While Insight aimed to recruit more female engineering professionals, the Girls and Technical Engineering (GATE) project launched in 1984 focused on recruiting technicians. This should not be confused with Girls and Technology Education, a separate project at Chelsea College which also used the acronym GATE. The EITB GATE project was a customised version of the Insight model, and consisted of courses at further education colleges which were targeted at fifth form girls who were not intending to stay on for the sixth form. The aims were to publicise career opportunities at technician and technician engineer levels and to increase the number of girls applying for technician training. As with Insight the programme made use of female technicians as group leaders and also included a day's visit to an engineering firm. In 1987 a work shadowing element was introduced and the college-based activities became more focused on hands-on problem solving (Engineering Industry Training Board, 1987, pp14-16). In 1987, the EITB claimed that it had been able to increase the numbers of young women entering technician training nationwide from one per cent in 1973 to 5.5 per cent in 1983 (Engineering Industry Training Board, 1987, p25). It is difficult to substantiate this claim since other factors such as other educational interventions, societal shifts and the women's movement also had some effect.

3. Into the 1990s: gender transformations in education?

The introduction of the National Curriculum through the Education Reform Act of 1988 was a key event in terms of gender and subject choice up to the age of sixteen. This core universal curriculum was part of a broader package of plans by the Conservative government to create a quasi-market in education: its purpose was partly to facilitate the process of making comparisons between the performance of pupils and schools (Brown, 2001, p175). Although gender equality was not a prominent consideration, the implementation of the National Curriculum played an important role in reducing the sex segregation of subjects at GCSE level so that by the mid-1990s, many of the differences between girls' and boys' educational trajectories up to this stage had substantially reduced (Francis, 2000). In 1994 compared with 1984 the dominance of boys in traditionally masculine subjects such as craft, design and technology and maths lessened, although they continued to be over-represented in physics, chemistry, and computer studies (Arnot et al, 1999, p20; Equal Opportunities Commission, 2002, p3).

However at A-level, in post-16 vocational education and in higher education, where a free choice of subjects continued, gender-segregated patterns persisted (Francis, 2000; Brown, 2001). In 1994 boys were still over-represented at A-level in maths, computer studies, economics, and craft, design and technology, and the gender gap had even increased in physics since 1984 (Arnot et al, 1999, p22). Vocational qualifications were also stratified by gender: young women chose qualifications in business and commerce, hairdressing and beauty and the caring services, while young men were more likely to choose science and engineering (Arnot et al, 1999, p22). In higher education with the exception of medical degrees, women remained concentrated in the arts and men in the sciences (Francis, 2000, p36). Furthermore, despite the narrowing of the gender gap in some subjects at GCSE, the introduction of the quasi-market in education was not a positive development in terms of equal opportunities as it required winners and losers and encouraged schools to select and invest in high achieving mainly white and middle-class students to the detriment of other groups (Apple, 2001; West and Pennell, 2002).

In the early 1990s the narrowing of gender gaps at GCSE led the EOC to conclude that its efforts had been successful and to decide that the provision of equality in education could now be left to the sector itself (Madden, 2000). However, the introduction of the education market and growth of new managerialist practices throughout the public sector during the 1980s meant that substantive progress on gender equality within school contexts was unlikely. Under the new public sector framework resources were diverted into meeting government targets and efficiency rather than equality became the order of the day (Apple, 2001). The prescriptive demands of National Curriculum left little space for curriculum innovations. As a result of this many gender equality projects died out and many LEAs dispensed with their Equal Opportunities Advisers (Madden, 2000). A rising moral panic about boys' underachievement, underlined by increasing zealousness around educational standards, made it difficult to institute reforms which were perceived to benefit girls (Francis, 1999).

4. Second Phase Projects

Despite these developments, by the mid-1990s an explicit central government concern with women's employment in SECT had begun to emerge. The policy debate was set in motion by perceived skills needs in SECT fields which it was believed could be met by unlocking women's under-used labour potential. The emergence of this business case for women's participation in SECT shifted the focus of activity to the Department of Trade and Industry and various large corporations rather than the education sector. Nevertheless, it was accompanied by a resurgence of educational initiatives targeted at girls and young women. The second phase of activity saw teachers at the grassroots taking less action because of the prescriptive nature of the National Curriculum and the increasing demands on teachers' time created by the managerialist culture. The relative decline of grassroots activity was accompanied by a growth in state and corporate funded initiatives which, perhaps because of the lack of input from teachers and academics, largely used simplistic first phase models and had little connection to contemporary developments in feminist theory and educational practice.

During this period government and industry set up various large SECT initiatives which were targeted at both girls and boys, reflecting the fact that applications to subjects such as physics and computing were dropping across the board (Institute of Physics, 2006). The government sponsored the SETPOINT scheme, which created regional agencies which were designed to provide support to teachers, schools and pupils in an effort to interest more young people in SECT. In the Science and Engineering Ambassadors programme SECT professionals visited local schools to work with pupils and serve as role models. In the mid-2000s there were plans to develop and run after-school science and engineering clubs (SETNET, 2007).

The Grow Your Own Workforce programme run by United Utilities and Scottish Power and supported by the North West Development Agency was another broad-based government and corporate initiative. So was the BAE Systems in School programme, a roadshow involving a theatre presentation and a workshop targeted at pupils aged 9 to 12 (BAE Systems, 2007). Such initiatives made use of the familiar model of awareness raising and hands-on experimentation which had characterised many first phase projects.

A more radical model underpinned one of the few grassroots interventions during the second phase: the Supported Learning in Physics Project (SLIPP) led by Elizabeth Whitelegg of the Open University between 1994 and 1999. This curriculum development initiative employed a context-based or humanistic approach and consisted of eight books of supported learning materials which embedded physics content in contextual case-studies. The Institute of Physics, the Institution of Mechanical Engineers, the Institution of Electrical Engineers and various commercial and industrial sponsors funded the project and Heinemann Educational published the books. Although the initiative was targeted at both sexes, Whitelegg attempted to make use of contextual settings which built on girls' interests as well as those of boys. For instance, the materials introduced the concept of equilibrium of forces through the context of rock climbing and used scuba diving as a context for the concept of pressure laws: both sports in which women and men were equally represented. Evaluation of the project showed that the girls felt that it aroused their interest and facilitated their understanding. However, the adoption of SLIPP materials was limited as it relied on teachers to make links to exam board specifications (Murphy and Whitelegg, 2006, p19).

Activities carried out at universities during the first phase of activity informed the setting up of the CREST (Creativity in Science and Technology) initiative. Launched in the mid-1980s, CREST was active throughout the second phase (personal communication). It allowed secondary school pupils to explore science and technology through hands-on activities conducted under the supervision of a mentor from academia or industry. Pupils could work towards an award at three different levels and present their work at regional fairs (Grant, 2006). Although the CREST scheme had no specific focus on gender it provided an umbrella for gender-based initiatives in which girls worked towards CREST awards, the most high profile of which was GETSET (Girls Entering Tomorrow's Science, Engineering and Technology). GETSET was launched as part of National Science Week in 1994 by CREST and Imperial College London and had a high profile patron in Johnny Ball. Companies such as British Telecom, Ford, IBM and Shell sponsored the project. GETSET enabled academically successful secondary school girls to work towards CREST awards during a three day course at a university. Team challenges were set around scenarios such as astronaut training, with women SECT professionals acting as mentors, role models and judges (British Association, 1994). By the late 1990s girls from 40 schools were participating in the project and by the early 2000s, when the project ended due to problems with maintaining funding, an average of 2000 girls were taking part each year (personal correspondence).

As well as the CREST and GETSET schemes, many individual first phase university initiatives continued into the second phase: these included day visits where schoolgirls met undergraduate students and academics, short courses involving hands-on experimentation and interaction with role models, lectures, careers advice and conferences for students, teachers and parents. The initiatives generally targeted girls studying for A-levels although some targeted younger girls. Institutions running such initiatives during the second phase included Imperial College, Shipley College in West Yorkshire, Hugh Baird College in Merseyside, Stow College in Glasgow, the Universities of Derby, Sussex, and Ulster, Queen Mary College at the University of London, City College London, Heriot-Watt University, and London Metropolitan University. Academics in some universities were also involved in outreach: in 1997 Alison Carter of the Engineering faculty at the University of Westminster extended an existing university outreach programme entitled Maths in Electronics to incorporate visits to maths classes in girls' schools to raise awareness of career opportunities in electronics and communications fields (personal correspondence).

Throughout the second phase of activity and due to a perennial shortage of student numbers in physics, the Institute of Physics was involved in various initiatives focused on both girls and boys. These included the creation of a physics teacher network and the production of resources for teaching physics both in the early years and at advanced level (Institute of Physics, 2007). The Institute published a critical review of research on the participation of girls in physics and a guide to inform teachers about why girls might choose not to study physics and to suggest strategies for tackling the problem, written by Patricia Murphy, Elizabeth Whitelegg, Martin Hollins and Bob Ponchaud (Murphy and Whitelegg, 2006; Institute of Physics, 2006a). They recommended teaching physics in a way that engaged the interest of both sexes, creating a classroom environment in which both girls and boys were expected to achieve, using constructivist and supportive teaching techniques, and emphasising the social contribution of physical science. Teachers TV made two videos to accompany the report (Institute of Physics, 2006a).

In the area of construction and the trades several initiatives were conducted in the 1990s and 2000s which focused on creating a more feminine or gender neutral image of the industry in order to attract young women. WARM (Women as Role Models) was set up in 1991 by women construction workers to raise the profile of women and to challenge the negative perceptions of construction believed to be held by girls and young women. Members worked with schools to run small-scale construction projects, careers talks and presentations and work experience placements in association with local companies (General NVQ, 1996, p17). In the mid-1990s the National Council for Vocational Qualifications and Department for Education and Employment embarked on a project focused on promoting the participation of young women in vocational qualifications in technology (GNVQs). This entailed two national conferences organised by the Construction Industry Training Board, a national seminar, and a series of posters intended to present a gender-neutral or feminine image of technology education (General NVQ, 1996). The Learning and Skills Council followed this in the early 2000s, collecting and publishing data on apprenticeships by sector, gender, race, and disability and considering ways in which young people could be encouraged to choose non-traditional career paths. As part of this initiative a marketing campaign was instituted to promote non-traditional areas of training and work (Women and Equality Unit, 2004).

Starting in the late 1990s the Let's TWIST project, led by Annette Williams at Bradford College, developed programmes for schoolgirls. The three day events and one day and two day workshops focused on raising girls' awareness of opportunities in fields such as engineering, surveying and bricklaying and giving them opportunities for hands-on experimentation. In the early 2000s the Let's TWIST-led JIVE partnership set up a work experience programme in the Yorkshire and Humber Region. Girls who had participated in Let's TWIST workshops were supported through work experience placements in SECT companies. Sheffield Hallam University delivered a similar programme under the JIVE banner entitled Wider Horizons. As the final component of the model JIVE outreach officer Helen Collier developed teacher training in gender equality with the involvement of local industry. The Let's TWIST projects were deemed successful in terms of female participants being offered apprenticeships and returning to placement venues for summer work. Girls and teachers gave positive feedback in informal evaluations. From the mid-2000s, efforts were made to encourage companies and schools to develop their own initiatives because of the time limited nature of the Let's TWIST and JIVE projects (personal communication).

In 2003 the JIVE partnership embarked on a new campaign with the EOC entitled Know Your Place. It aimed to encourage girls to consider a career in the construction, engineering, information technology and plumbing industries and used posters, leaflets, and a website with information and case studies of women who had experience of training or working in these areas. Between 2003 and 2005 the EOC conducted research into why women and men continued to work in traditional jobs and why young people chose apprenticeships and other vocational training in traditional sectors. The research focused on areas with skills shortages: construction, engineering, plumbing, information and communication technology, and childcare. A youth focused website entitled Works4me followed, to raise awareness of career opportunities amongst 11-15 year-olds. The website contained a virtual careers centre with features such as games, quizzes, animation and music and information about pay scales, qualifications, work experience and employers (Equal Opportunities Commission, 2006).

Also in the early 2000s the Construction Industry Training Board (CITB) embarked on a series of school visits and a national publicity campaign targeted at girls and ethnic minority pupils (Pillbeam and Farren, 2004, p16). A dedicated Women's Campaign was launched in 2004 to raise awareness of construction careers and improve the industry's image, aimed at girls aged 10-14 and those influencing them such as their parents, teachers and careers advisers. Alongside this school-based project, B Constructive was used as an umbrella for the production of educational materials and informational literature for schools and Connexions careers offices (Pillbeam and Farren, 2004, p16). By 2006 the CITB's equal opportunities policy involved a partnership with the Construction Youth Trust for promoting the participation of women and ethnic minorities, diversity and awareness training at the National Construction College, a Positive Image campaign of publicity and literature featuring women and ethnic minorities. It had a target of 30 per cent women and 10 per cent ethnic minority representation for its Construction Ambassadors who visited schools (Construction Industry Training Board, 2006).

In 1999 the national IMAGE initiative was launched by e-skills UK, a not-for-profit employer-led organisation supported by the Department of Trade and Industry with a brief to ensure that the UK had the skills needed to compete in the global economy (e-skills UK, 2007). IMAGE aimed to change the image of ICT held by adolescent girls through a national PR campaign and workshops in schools. As part of this initiative the organisation set up the project IT Beat, which focused on changing girls' perceptions of ICT and developing their computing skills. IT Beat featured a competition in 2002 in which girls designed a website for their favourite pop star: the winners were invited to meet pop stars and other celebrities at a so-called slumber party at the Science Museum in London in 2003. The idea was to infuse ICT with an aura of glamour and fun to counteract the geeky image thought to be off-putting to the broad mass of girls (Preston and MacKeogh, 2003, p41; Pitt, 2003a). However, the success of the initiative in altering girls' understandings of ICT was difficult to measure, and although IT Beat was originally intended to be an annual event, it had died out by the mid-2000s (Pitt, 2003a).

Case Study 3.3: Computer clubs for girls

In 2002 e-skills UK set up the Computer Clubs for Girls (CC4G) project with funding from the Department for Education and Skills, an example of the collaboration between state and industry which characterised the second phase of activity. CC4G started as a pilot at 24 schools in the South East of England, and by 2006 2200 schools were participating in the project. The objective was for the schools to develop and deliver lunchtime or after-school workshops in computing for girls at Key Stage 2 and 3 who were between the ages of 10 and 14, using software provided by e-skills UK. Teachers, teaching assistants, after-school co-ordinators and senior students received training materials to help them to facilitate the clubs. In 2005 the organisation set up links with local employers who were willing to arrange site visits for girls or to provide volunteers to assist with workshops (personal correspondence). CC4G could be seen as a formalised national version of some of the grassroots computing initiatives set up during the first phase of activity and in adult education in the 1970s and 80s (see Chapter Five), but it had few similarities with these more radical interventions.

CC4G software was accessed via the Internet, and the materials were designed to complement the national curriculum at Key Stages 2 and 3. The focus was on developing capability and confidence in technology rather than on specific skills and the project emphasised the so-called soft skills such as teamwork and communication, which became increasingly attractive to employers as they became increasingly tied to profit from the 1990s onwards (Mitter, 1995). The model was familiar, working at the level of girls' attitudes and choices: the main aims were to change their perceptions of ICT as a difficult and boring subject and to 'present a whole new range of prospective careers that they might not have considered' (e-skills UK, 2006, p2). The twelve modules of the curriculum aimed to make ICT more girl friendly by presenting it through topics such as celebrity, fashion, dance, music and games. Each topic made use of a different skill such as desktop publishing, data gathering, handling and presentation and designing and creating software. Girls were encouraged to work at their own pace and to ask for help when they needed it (personal correspondence).

An internal evaluation of CC4G carried out in August 2005 cited the growing scale of the project as a sign of its success, reporting that a total of 8611 girls were registered as club participants at 314 schools. Quantitative evaluation was undertaken using questionnaires targeted at both the girls and the 513 registered facilitators. The facilitators' responses were overwhelmingly positive: 97 per cent reported that the girls' confidence levels in ICT had improved, 96 per cent thought that the girls' skill levels in ICT had improved, and 99 per cent thought that the girls would achieve better results at Key Stage 3 as a result of their experience in the clubs. The questionnaires completed by the girls evoked a mixed response: 66 per cent thought that they were more likely to work in a technology-related career because of their participation in the clubs but only 35 per cent had been able to apply their new knowledge and skills to settings outside the clubs. The most positive response concerned continued participation: 92 per cent of the girls planned to remain members during the next school year (personal correspondence). In terms of its scale CC4G was an ambitious initiative and might well have raised awareness of the issue of girls and ICT at national level. However, it necessitated a superficial and generic approach based on providing supplementary technological solutions from a distance rather than engaging with classroom dynamics, the mainstream curriculum and the formation of girls' gender identities in relation to SECT.

Case Study 3.4: Women Into Science and Engineering
The Women Into Science and Engineering (WISE) Campaign is arguably the best known and best funded initiative focused on girls' experience of and participation in SECT and endured largely unchanged throughout both phases of activity. Founded by Marie-Noëlle Barton, it was launched by Margaret Thatcher during WISE Year in 1984, and funded by the Engineering Council and the EOC. By the early 2000s the campaign had secured funding from three of the four major national bodies for engineering: the Engineering Technology Board (previously the Engineering Council), the Engineering Employers' Federation, and the Sector Skills Council for Science, Engineering, and Manufacturing Technologies (personal communication). It also received funding from the Department of Trade and Industry and various UK corporations (Women into Science and Engineering Campaign, 2006b). Because of this flow of funding, the campaign can be viewed as being employer driven and corporate rather than education focused. Throughout its

long history it became well established, and disseminated its message through its head office in London and regional committees of volunteers in Wales, Northern Ireland and Scotland (personal communication).

WISE was certainly a key carrier of the dominant framework focused on influencing girls' perceptions of SECT and encouraging them to make different educational and career choices (Henwood, 1996). The scale and visibility of the campaign throughout the two phases of activity helped to establish this deficit model of girls as received wisdom among many policy makers, teachers, researchers and activists. WISE activities within this framework included political lobbying, producing print and multimedia materials for parents, teachers and schoolgirls, collating a yearly Directory of Initiatives and raising awareness through events and conferences. Its major educational project was the WISE Bus, which began operating in 1984 as a mobile classroom which offered girls the opportunity to explore technology at their own pace and in a single-sex environment. Up to six buses, with a variety of equipment installed, visited schools throughout England for periods from a few days up to a month. Each bus was customised to accommodate groups of up to 16 girls aged 13 and 14, who took part in 90 minute workshop sessions, supervised by their teachers. The equipment on the bus allowed pupils to work on topics such as mechanisms, microelectronics, pneumatics, microprocessors, computer-aided design and communications (personal communication).

The WISE Bus project aimed to improve girls' confidence around technology and arouse their interest in technical subjects and careers. A comprehensive longitudinal evaluation would have been necessary to assess its benefits fully, but a small-scale independent evaluation conducted at two schools in 2003 suggested that it provided a positive – though brief – change from the participants' normal science and technology classes. Sixty four girls completed multiple-choice questionnaires and fourteen were selected for in-depth interviews about their experience of the project. Although the girls reported that they had enjoyed the workshops, many were unsure about what they had learned and how their experience might shape their education and future plans. Many were interested in stereotypically feminine disciplines and professions such as childcare, humanities and the performing arts and none felt that they were more likely to pursue a career in SECT as a result of their time on the WISE Bus (Phipps, 2005).

In 2005 the Wise Bus project was discontinued and replaced by WISE Outlook, which had been running for some time on a smaller scale and consisted of three day courses for girls aged 13 and 14 at schools, colleges, universities and SETPOINTS sponsored by the Engineering Employers' Federation. WISE Outlook was targeted at high-achieving girls who were good candidates for technical professions and aimed to influence their subject and career choices through giving them an opportunity to experience engineering at first hand. The girls took part in hands-on design projects, met women students and staff from technical colleges and interacted with role models who were professional women engineers (personal communication). The WISE Outlook model arguably had more depth and potential than the WISE Bus because it was delivered through three days of intensive and varied activity. But WISE Outlook was based on the familiar deficit model of its female participants, problematising their perceptions and choices and asking them to embrace the profession of engineering unconditionally, without engaging with its masculine structures, cultures and practices.

Feminists criticised WISE from its inception for uncritically attempting to draw women into male-dominated and masculine fields (Ferry, 1985; Henwood, 1996) but these criticisms did not appear to affect the development of the WISE model, which remained largely unchanged for two decades. In 2006 WISE claimed that its initiatives had helped to increase the number of female engineering graduates in the UK from 7 per cent in 1984 to more than 18 per cent in 2006 (Women into Science and Engineering Campaign, 2006b). This claim is difficult to substantiate due to the lack of in-depth and longitudinal evaluation of WISE initiatives and the complex interaction of factors structuring girls' and women's subject choices. At the very least WISE had a broad and positive impact in raising awareness of the issue of women's participation in SECT on a national level and provided a visible brand and umbrella for grassroots activists, which many made use of even while simultaneously questioning the campaign's framework. Having institutionalised the WISE brand and attracted patrons such as HRH The Princess Royal and Baroness Platt of Writtle, WISE founder Marie-Noëlle Barton handed over leadership to Terry Marsh in the mid-2000s.

This heralded the dawn of a new era for WISE, with a focus on science and technology literacy for the broad mass of girls which took place alongside a steady shift away from the deficit model in policy circles (personal communication).

Case Study 3.5: Gender and Science and Technology (GASAT)
The Girls and Science and Technology (GASAT) Association was founded in 1981 and was still extant in the mid-2000s spanning both phases of activity. Jan Harding of Chelsea College and Jan Raat, Head of Physics Education at Eindhoven University, set up GASAT as a network to facilitate the exchange of information and ideas amongst academics and teachers. The key settings for this interaction were international and regional conferences which attracted participants from a wide range of countries including Australia, Canada, China, Denmark, England, Germany, Ghana, Italy, India, Israel, Kenya, Malaysia, Mauritius, Norway, the Netherlands, Nigeria, the Philippines, Spain, Sweden and the US (Lie, 1983; Craig and Harding, 1985). From its inception GASAT had a predominant focus on science and technology education for girls but concerns with supporting female students in universities and women working in scientific and technological fields grew as the association developed. In addition and alongside increasing representation from the global South, the theme of science and technology for sustainable development became more significant. The association's twelfth international conference, held in Brighton in 2006, centred on the interactions between science and technology and the United Nations millennium development goals (personal communication).

Unusually, GASAT operated as a multi-disciplinary partnership between academic natural and social scientists and science educators. This involved attempts to foster dialogue between qualitative and quantitative researchers and to make connections between theory and practice. This work was influenced by feminist ideas, in particular a rejection of the deficit model of girls and women and an effort to examine the ideologies, knowledge structures and cultures of science and technology in a critical way. The early GASAT model, as articulated by Harding, was based on the interactions between the philosophy, aims and organisation of education, the practice of science and technology, and the assumptions made about appropriate male and female behaviour (Raat, Harding and Mottier, 1981a; personal communication). This focus on deconstructing science and technology and their interaction with gender marks GASAT as more radical than many contemporaneous initiatives. At the fourth international conference in the US it was agreed to change the name of GASAT to the Gender and Science and Technology Association to reflect this analytical framework, although there was resistance from some members motivated by fears of being seen as too openly feminist (personal communication).

The first GASAT conference was held in 1981 at the Eindhoven University of Technology, funded by the Dutch government. It was attended by twenty Dutch science educators and twenty researchers from overseas, with sub-groups focused on teacher education, support for women, and curricula and teaching materials (Raat, Harding and Mottier, 1981b). The second conference was held at the University of Oslo in 1983 and incorporated workshops on sex stereotypes and interaction, the curriculum, intervention programmes and teacher education (Lie, 1983). London was the setting for the third conference in 1985, which was based on the themes of technology education, strategies for change, and women, society, science and technology, with special interest groups on history and sociology (Craig and Harding, 1985). Further international conferences were held approximately every two years in the US, Israel, Australia, Canada, India, Ghana, Denmark, Mauritius and the UK. GASAT also provided an umbrella for smaller regional conferences bringing together researchers from Europe, Africa, and Australasia. Conference organisers blended the intellectual and the social, usually providing some form of social activity and cultural exchange.

Despite the association's relatively sophisticated approach, many of the papers presented at GASAT conferences cleaved to the dominant deficit model of girls and young women and focused on strategies such as awareness raising and changing the image of science. However, there were notable exceptions, including the presentations given at GASAT 2 by John Head which focused on object relations theory and adolescent subject choice, and by Valerie Walkerdine who deconstructed the gendering of rationality and how it affected assessments of girls' mathematics performance (Head, 1983; Walkerdine, 1983). Several conferences in the 1980s were also attended by members of the Australian McClintock collective, a network of science educators who were engaged in developing context-based and socially relevant science curricula and creative teaching methods (Hildebrand, 1989). At the 1992 regional conference in Eindhoven Carrie Paechter presented her work on power and gender in the design and technology curriculum and a group of academics from the Open University reported on a pilot study around gender and collaborative work in primary classrooms (Paechter, 1992; Whitelegg, Murphy, Scanlon and Hodgson, 1992). Throughout the conferences there was discussion of issues such as science and militarism, technology and social responsibility, developments in feminist literature around science and technology, feminist pedagogy and the possibility of a feminist science (personal communication).

It is clear that the GASAT model was both sophisticated and radical when compared with many of the other initiatives operating in both phases of activity. Its internationalism and practices of partnership between academics and educators fostered much productive dialogue. However, by the time of GASAT 11 in Mauritius in 2003 some participants felt that much of the discussion had become mired in old-fashioned and atheoretical frameworks which were concerned with simple access to SECT rather than transformation of its cultures and practices and which made use of essentialist constructions of gender (Parker, 2003). This perhaps reflected the dominance of state and corporate actors in setting the agenda for the second phase of activity and the wider backlash against feminism and social justice projects which characterised the period. Nevertheless, on the whole GASAT conferences provided a supportive and stimulating venue for the discussion of imaginative and potentially transformative approaches to gender and SECT education.

5. Discussion

A variety of initiatives were put in place between the 1970s and the mid-2000s which focused on girls' and young women's achievements in science and technology education and subsequent subject and career choices. Within the pre-1988 decentralised education system the grass-roots activities of feminist teachers had an impact in terms of challenging traditional gender roles and experimenting with radical pedagogy and curricula (Arnot *et al*, 1999, p151). However, the major aim of altering girls' subject choices was more difficult to achieve and although some progress was made the gendering of physical science and technology subjects persisted. By 1987 girls were achieving only 28 per cent of passes at O-level and 21 per cent of passes at A-level physics, and in chemistry achieved 41 per cent and 37 per cent of passes at O- and A-level respectively (Baronness Platt of Writtle, 1988, p644). Applications for degrees in subjects such as physics and computing were dropping generally but particularly from young women. Initiatives put in place during the second phase of activity in the mid-1990s were restricted by the post-1988 managerialism and centralised control of the school curriculum. The strategies employed were much the same as those developed during the first phase, with little apparent reflection on possible areas for improvement despite the slow pace of change.

By the early 2000s progress had been made in terms of girls' representation in some school subjects due to the introduction of the national curriculum and undoubtedly because of the projects described here. However, although by academic year 2003/04 girls were better represented than boys in the now compulsory GCSE maths and new integrated science courses, boys continued to dominate design and technology subjects such as electronics, graphics, resistant materials and systems control. As shown in Table 3.2 below, girls were

---

Table 3.2 A level entries in maintained institutions in England and Wales by gender and subject, 2004

	Per cent boys	Per cent girls
Biological sciences	39	61
Chemistry	49	51
Physics	80	20
Mathematics	63	37
Design and Technology	60	40
Computer Studies	90	10
ICT	65	35

(UK Resource Centre for Women in SET, 2005)

---

over-represented in biological sciences and had achieved equal representation in chemistry, but remained a minority at A-level in physics,
mathematics, design and technology, computer studies and ICT.

At degree level women were by then the majority of undergraduate students overall and were over-represented in fields such as education,
sociology, languages and biological sciences. Men continued to
dominate physical and mathematical sciences, computer science,
economics, and engineering and technology (UK Resource Centre for
Women in SET, 2005b).

The relatively slow progress in altering girls' and young women's subject
choices is due in part to the difficulty of intervening on the complex
interaction of social, cultural, educational and psychological factors
which structured them. But it is also necessary to examine the projects
themselves, particularly the predominant model which situated girls as
the problem and attempted to alter their perceptions and choices without engaging with the contexts in which these were formed and made.
Although more critical and radical interpretations were in evidence,
particularly at the grassroots and embodied by the GASAT Association,
a central assumption for many projects was that girls and women were
opting out of SECT subjects because they – wrongly – perceived SECT
to be masculine and because their feminine socialisation made them
unable to challenge gender stereotypes. This deficit model of girls and
young women inspired compensatory strategies intended to help
female students to participate and achieve in science and technology,
while the subjects themselves were left unchallenged and unaltered.

The focus on changing girls' and young women's socialised aptitudes,
skills, and identities was positive in avoiding the biological determinism that had historically positioned girls as fundamentally incapable of performing in SECT (Manthorpe, 1987). However, this approach operated at the level of the individual rather than that of context
and structure and inspired largely superficial strategies. The idea of girl-
friendly science, or of creating a science compatible with socialised
femininity, involved changing how the subject was presented so that it
appealed to girls' interests rather than examining the content of the
curriculum, the nature of scientific epistemologies and methodologies
and the masculine structures and cultures of SECT. There were excep-

tions in projects such as Jan Harding's Chemistry from Issues course or Elizabeth Whitelegg's SLIPP intervention, which involved a thorough recontextualisation of the science curriculum, focusing on issues of interest to both boys and girls rather than using isolated and supposedly feminine teaching examples. Unfortunately, the propagation of these ideas was hindered by the prescriptive demands of the school curriculum.

Awareness raising strategies were used to alter girls' and young women's so-called misperceptions of the masculinity of SECT and to introduce them to the possibilities of SECT education and careers. Such strategies were often simplistic: the popular practice of role modelling was based on the assumption that interacting with one successful female SECT professional was enough to inspire girls to reject powerfully gendered social processes and structures (Byrne, 1993, p88). These approaches were overly deterministic, objectifying girls and young women and failing to give them enough credit for exercising agency in their interactions and choices (Volman *et al*, 1995, p290). The growing body of evidence around the structural, cultural and symbolic masculinities of SECT did not seem to lead to a general questioning about whether girls and young women were actually making sensible decisions in their rejection of possible careers in these fields (see also Henwood, 1996).

It is useful to question whether the idea of girl-friendly science helped to challenge gender stereotypes or whether it reiterated essentialist constructions of femininity which, historically, had been used to keep women out of SECT. Altering the presentation of SECT subjects in line with themes such as social and environmental issues or the human body implicitly located girls as synonymous with social interests and skills while boys were identified with technical interests and skills (Phipps, 2005). The focus on hands-on experimentation rather than working from abstract scientific concepts reflected the historical positioning of women as incapable of abstract rationality (Faulkner, 2001; Gilbert, 2001; Hughes, 2001). More overtly, some projects such as Computer Clubs for Girls attempted to arouse girls' interest in SECT subjects by presenting them through examples such as celebrity, dance, and fashion. Such constructions may well have undermined the broader political messages of the projects by reinforcing the gender stereotypes they intended to challenge (Phipps, 2007).

Projects in both phases were short-term and sporadic in nature due to erratic flows of funding and were frequently positioned as a supplement to the mainstream educational process. This was largely because of the limited and limiting context in which they operated, which inhibited longitudinal interventions and in which challenges to the mainstream curriculum were increasingly difficult to make. Throughout both phases of activity central government support was restricted by cuts in spending on social justice projects which characterised both Conservative and New Labour administrations. The introduction of the National Curriculum in 1988 and an increasingly managerialist culture in education prevented many teachers from engaging in radical activities. Also, the emergent moral panic around boys' underachievement which began to dominate the educational agenda acted as a damper on reforms perceived to be for the benefit of girls, particularly when coupled with the social and cultural backlash against feminism (Skelton, 1998; Francis, 1999; Faludi, 1992; Callaghan *et al*, 1999; Hawkesworth, 1999). As a result of all this girls and young women continued to struggle unseen against discrimination in educational contexts (Warrington and Younger, 2000).

Thus it is easy to see how projects which sought to change individual girls rather than engaging with the institutions, cultures and knowledge structures of SECT were often the only possible model. Such projects had many positive results, particularly in terms of raising political and social awareness and providing an umbrella for various types of feminist activism. However, it was difficult if not impossible for such individualistic, short term and supplementary interventions to create the dramatic changes which were hoped for. To achieve such transformations, it would have been necessary to engage with the co-construction of gender and SECT within mainstream education. Pupils could have been asked to consider how SECT and masculinity were mutually constitutive, and to discuss how this disadvantaged both girls and boys. Humanistic, context-based approaches to teaching could have been used as a model for a wholesale re-contextualisation of the science and technology curriculum to engage with the interests of both genders. Some work of this nature was undertaken at the grassroots during both phases, and feminist ideas and educational practice were brought together under the banner of the GASAT Association. However, in 2007 it is difficult to imagine how such initiatives could be expanded within the rigid curriculum and managerial structures of British education.

4

Supporting women in a chilly climate
Projects for female SECT professionals

The under-representation of girls and women in SECT education at school and college clearly affected their ability to pursue SECT subjects in higher education and their subsequent representation among workers in SECT professions. Although women were an increasing proportion of higher education students from the 1970s, their participation and levels of advancement in SECT subjects and professions remained low. Attrition particularly tended to occur at postgraduate and higher faculty levels and the upper levels of SECT industries such as senior management. There was a significant gender pay gap and few women were members of SECT professional societies (Greenfield *et al*, 2002; Anderson and Connolly, 2006). Formalised activity among women SECT professionals started in the early twentieth century and from the 1980s a growing number of groups emerged which were focused on helping and encouraging female SECT students and supporting and advancing women in SECT professions. This chapter describes some of these groups, exploring their structures and main activities and commenting on what they achieved in the often rigid and restricting context of SECT disciplines and professions.

1. Setting the scene: women in SECT professions

Table 4.1 shows that although women were well represented among undergraduate students in medical, dental and health disciplines (including nursing) and over-represented in arts, languages and literature by 1984, they were under-represented in science subjects and significantly under-represented in engineering and technology. At post-graduate level women were in a minority across the board, even in subjects such as languages and literature which they dominated at undergraduate level.

Table 4.1 Qualifications attained on higher education courses by level and subject area 1984

Subject	Undergraduate % Women	Postgraduate % Women
Languages and literature	70	44
Arts	56	29
Medical, dental, health	49	38
Science	34	22
Engineering and technology	7	8

(Breakwell, 1986, p30, table 2)

Table 4.2 Employment by major sector by sex 1983

Sector	% Women
Services	63
Distribution, hotels, catering	54
Banking and finance	49
Agriculture, forestry and fisheries	25
Engineering and vehicle manufacturing	21
Mining and metal manufacturing	20
Transport and communications	20
Energy and water supply	13
Construction	12

(Breakwell, 1986, p29, table 1)

In terms of employment, in the early 1980s women constituted 40 per cent of the overall labour force. Table 4.2 shows that they were not evenly distributed across the various sectors: although they constituted a majority of service sector employees they were a minority in other fields and a small minority in fields such as engineering and vehicle manufacturing, mining and metal manufacturing, transport and communications, energy and water supply and construction.

The reasons for attrition in SECT education and inequality in the SECT workplace were often put down to a so-called 'chilly climate' (Hall and Sandler, 1982) in which the policies and practices of SECT workplaces did not accommodate the realities of women workers' lives and gendered perceptions of ambitions and skills undermined women's efforts (Greenfield *et al*, 2002). The chilly climate included horizontal and vertical segregation in which women were over-represented in non-technical sectors of SECT and under-represented at the higher levels of all sectors, a structural problem which was one of the causes of the gender pay gap. There were also elements specific to SECT companies such as inadequate provision of maternity and paternity leave or of flexible working and childcare, difficulties for women returning to work after career breaks, masculine workplace cultures seen in the types of social activities chosen, long working hours, requirements for frequent travel and the prevalence of short-term contact working. Some aspects were related to overt prejudice evidenced in discrimination in recruitment and funding decisions, sexual harassment and bullying and sexist assumptions made about women's abilities (Prentice, 2000; Bebbington, 2002; Ellis, 2003; Athena Project, 2005).

Between the 1980s and the 2000s groups and organisations were set up to support women working in SECT and to help them survive and thrive in the chilly climate. Independent or attached to universities and professional institutions, they took various forms such as membership organisations for women professionals, face-to-face or Internet networks, women's groups within professional associations and formal or informal initiatives in universities to support female staff and students. Strategies included formal and informal mentoring, seminars and conferences, workshops for skills development, networking and lobbying corporations and government around issues such as flexible working and childcare. Courses were set up to help women returners to update their skills and to ease the transition back into work. The majority of these groups were founded during the 1990s and 2000s, coinciding with the emergence of corporate and governmental concerns about skills shortages in SECT fields and the spread of Internet technologies.

2. Membership organisations

Membership organisations were an early form of action targeted at women in SECT professions. They usually operated via a head office and local chapters. Women SECT professionals were normally charged a subscription fee in return for being provided with various services. Networking was organised via physical meetings or online discussion forums or email lists, for the purposes of support, discussion of issues relevant to women in SECT and making professional contacts. Databases of contacts were produced for women members, and newsletters and web portals kept them updated on relevant events and developments within SECT and publicised job opportunities. Mentoring was a central strategy and involved senior women supporting those at earlier stages in their careers. Events were run with guest speakers, usually successful senior women in SECT, and skills workshops were provided for women members. The conferences focused either on the theme of women's participation in SECT or on topics specific to SECT disciplines, and publications were produced for dissemination to policy-makers, women members and the general public. Some groups engaged in outreach activities such as careers taster days for schoolgirls and awareness raising amongst parents and teachers. Funding was provided for small events organised by members or for individual members to attend conferences when no funds were available from their employers. Some groups lobbied central government and corporations about working conditions for women in SECT and contributed to policy discussions, although this was fairly rare.

One of the first such membership organisations was the National Association of Women Pharmacists (NAWP), founded in 1905. As well as the usual activities the association ran weekend courses which were specifically targeted at women returning from career breaks and these pre-dated most other initiatives for women returners (National Association of Women Pharmacists, 2003). NAWP also conducted small-scale research on topics such as the pharmacy workforce and developed a career pack for women pharmacists (Association for Women in Science and Engineering, 2001c). Women's progress in pharmacy throughout the twentieth century was better than in other scientific disciplines. By 2001 women made up half the members of the Royal Pharmaceutical Society and 60 per cent of pharmacy graduates, and NAWP had broadened its remit to lobby on behalf of women as receivers of health care (Association for Women in Science and Engineering, 2001c).

The Women's Engineering Society (WES) was founded in 1919 (see case study 4.1). The British Federation of Business and Professional Women was founded in 1935 under the leadership of WES organising secretary Caroline Haslett. The Federation grew out of the British Federation of Business and Professional Women's Clubs, a predominantly social organisation, but in contrast had the explicitly political aim of lobbying for women's employment rights while not looking 'too feministic' (Perriton, 2007, p85). Unlike other membership organisations, its central strategy was to lobby the mainstream political establishment. This it did through letter-writing, holding meetings, and building links with mainly Conservative women MPs who were sympathetic to its campaign in the interests of the professional middle classes. It also had an international focus, linking with the International Federation of Business and Professional Women which was formed in 1930. The Federation's political engagement was at its height during the post-war debates on equal pay and by 1951 it represented 90,000 women in Britain. But by 1959 it was in financial crisis due to decreasing membership and a lack of volunteers, and it was dissolved in 1969. The Federation of Business and Professional Women's Clubs continued into the 2000s as UK Business and Professional Women Ltd (Perriton, 2007).

After the World Wars it appears that no membership organisations specific to women in SECT professions were formed until the 1980s, when a significant number of membership organisations for female SECT professionals emerged, inspired perhaps by the activities of the second wave women's movement. Women into Computing (WiC) was founded in 1984 during a meeting of academics at Edinburgh University (see also Chapter Three). The group was a collaboration between academics from computing and the social sciences and was unusual in being loosely organised as a feminist collective: a wide range of views were expressed including socialist, lesbian-feminist and black feminist perspectives. The group tried to build links with the mainstream computer science community and regularly lobbied the Committee of Heads and Professors of Computing (CPHC), although WiC was seen by some within the mainstream as too strident and politically motivated. WiC began to decline in the mid-2000s because of outside pressures on participants and a dwindling supply of new members. The last WiC conference was held at Greenwich University in July 2005, after which the group officially disbanded (personal correspondence).

In 1987 architect Elspeth Clements and chartered surveyor Michelle Foster set up the Association of Women in Property and by the early 2000s it had 1500 members nationwide (Women in Property, 2007). The early 1990s saw a renewed phase of government and corporate interest in the issue of women in SECT and the emergence of a number of groups. In 1992, the Women in Construction Alliance (WICA) was formed by a group of female architects (Women in Construction Alliance, 1994; personal communication). Academic chemist Joan Mason founded the Association for Women in Science and Engineering (AWiSE) in 1994 after being involved in producing the government report *The Rising Tide* (see Chapter Six). This report put forward the business case for women's equality and highlighted a need for net-working and mutual support. At the same time that the Department of Trade and Industry created a Promoting SET for Women Unit, AWiSE was launched to support women in SECT professions and promote the participation of girls and young women in SECT (personal communica-tion). AWiSE thrived for about ten years but after Joan Mason died in 2004 the national association lost its momentum. The Cambridge branch remained active and subsequently expanded to represent women scientists beyond the Cambridgeshire region (Cambridge AWiSE, 2007).

In 1999 Women in Architecture evolved from the informal Women's Architecture Group which had been in existence since 1985, creating a formal space for women architects to meet, support each other and en-gage in various activities (Women in Architecture, 2007). The National Association of Women in Construction was founded in 2002 by a group of female construction professionals led by Lorraine Elliot (National Association of Women in Construction, 2007). In 2000 DigitalEve was created by technology professionals Dana Jones, Diane Darling and Judy Hawkins to support women who were interested in online technologies as possible fields of study and work or as tools for everyday life. By 2001 the group had over 20,000 members, corporate sponsorship, and eight directors located in Boston, Chicago, San Francisco, Seattle, Toronto and London. The UK chapter dissolved in the mid-2000s although the international organisation remained active (DigitalEve, 2007).

Case study 4.1: the Women's Engineering Society
The Women's Engineering Society (WES) was set up in 1919 by Lady Katherine Parsons, a keen amateur engineer, her daughter Rachel Parsons, a qualified engineer, Margaret Lady Moir of Women Engineering Relief Workers, propeller gluer Verena Holmes and electrical engineer Margaret Partridge who owned a power station. These women decided to confront the threat to the continued employment of women engineers who had made a huge contribution to the war effort. In the face of opposition to women's employment from the government, industry and trades unions, they aimed to support trained women engineers and to help them exchange ideas on developments in their discipline, further training, and job opportunities. Under the leadership of organising secretary Caroline Haslett, the first issue of the WES magazine *The Woman Engineer* appeared in 1919 and by 1920 six regional branches had been formed. The first annual conference was held in 1923 in Birmingham. In its early stages the Society struggled to make any headway since although many professional institutions had begun to admit women, their progress in education and training remained slow and the 1930s depression caused high unemployment – a further deterrent to the employment of women. By the 1930s some WES branches had begun to lose momentum (Hatfield, 2005; personal communication).

Before the Second World War aviation became a new opportunity area for women. An aeronautical section of WES was launched under the leadership of President and pilot Amy Johnson and the British Women Pilots' Association was formed in 1957. During the Second World War women were again needed in the workplace, and Caroline Haslett was appointed as an adviser to the Ministry of Labour. Membership of WES rose to almost 300 women and the branches revived, although peace in 1945 brought a return of the marriage bar to many professions. Between 1946 and 1969 WES developed international links, participated in the annual Engineering Exhibition at Olympia and initiated the first two International Conferences of Women Engineers and Scientists in New York in 1964 and Cambridge in 1967 with the US Society of Women Engineers. The 50th birthday of the Society saw 1969 designated Women in Engineering Year during a second wave of radical feminist activism (Hatfield, 2005; personal communication).

The 1970s and 1980s brought financial problems for WES and other voluntary groups as increasingly powerful neo-liberal ideologies and policies reduced funding for social justice projects. But awareness of the need for women's skills in the developing knowledge economy increased and WES registered its first corporate members and set up student groups. Women into Science and Engineering year in 1984 reflected the heightened official interest in women's contribution to Britain's scientific and technical development. By then membership of the Society had reached 800, and it became a registered charity in 1985. As feminist politics fragmented in the 1990s, the branches again declined, but circles were set up as an informal alternative, representing the North West, Surrey and Sussex, Scotland, London and the Heart of England. These groups of members organised social events and technical networking. Informal student groups were also set up, and by the mid-2000s there were groups at the Universities of Lancaster and Surrey and University College London, although the pattern of universities involved constantly shifted (Hatfield, 2005; personal communication).

By the mid-2000s WES had around 700 registered individual members, mostly practising women engineers working in industry but also academics in related fields, women on career breaks, school and college students considering careers in engineering, retired women engineers and a few interested men. WES managed to enlist a number of corporate members including BBC Technologies, the Esso and Exxon Group, Jaguar, Unilever plc, the Ministry of Defence and Hewlett Packard, although these members came and went with shifting corporate priorities. The Institution of Electrical Engineers, which became the Institution of Engineering and Technology, was for many years a consistent sponsor. *The Woman Engineer*, produced quarterly since 1919, was still being published and carried articles of technical interest, reports on Society activities and national and international concerns and profiles of women engineers. The annual conferences had continued, incorporating talks and workshops on working life, specialist discussion of topics in engineering, and opportunities for networking and informal mentoring. The conferences and some local activities were approved for Continuing Professional Development purposes by most of the national professional engineering institutions. WES remained centrally involved with the series of international conferences for women engineers and scientists and with the International Network of Women Engineers and Scientists (Women's Engineering Society, 2007; personal communication).

During the 2000s WES supported a wide range of initiatives in engineering and provided a voice for women in the industry, expert speakers for schools and careers conventions and expert input to government and other policy-making bodies. The Society was closely associated with many projects including the independent Daphnet email list for women in science, engineering and technology, which carried news and information about issues, initiatives and job openings for women in SECT. WES also owned the MentorSET project, a formal mentoring scheme launched in 2002 in partnership with AWiSE. The project's central remit was to provide mentoring for women who might otherwise be isolated, such as those who worked in small to medium-sized enterprises with few other female employees and few resources. The intention was to facilitate mentoring partnerships between more and less experienced women and to support these partners during the mentoring process by providing guidelines and training. By the mid-2000s the project had brought together more than 300 mentoring pairs across the UK and had a number of affiliated groups including Cambridge AWiSE, the Women in Physics Group at the Institute of Physics, BCSWomen, the Daphne Jackson Trust, and Women@CL in Cambridge. Financial sponsorship was provided by the UK Resource Centre for Women in Science, Engineering and Technology and the mentors and other volunteers freely gave of their time (MentorSET, 2006; Women's Engineering Society, 2007; personal communication).

3. Networking groups
Alongside more structured membership organisations, informal networks for women in SECT may have existed since women first began to participate in the professions. But there is scant information about

these networks before the mid 1980s, when records of meetings and copies of group newsletters survived. Unlike membership organisations, such networks did not usually charge their members a fee: this possibly restricted their activities to those which could be carried out without much funding. The networks operated via physical meetings and online discussion lists and web portals through which women members shared ideas, supported each other and were provided with information about events and job opportunities. Some networks also engaged in outreach to schoolgirls and supported women SECT students at universities. There was little lobbying of the mainstream political establishment and corporations, perhaps due to the informal nature of the networks.

One of the few examples of networks active in the 1980s is feminist collective Women for Science for Women, founded in 1985 by research biologist Linda Birke and Gail Vines, New Scientist feature editor. As well as producing a newsletter, they made an unsuccessful attempt to set up a physical Women and Science Centre in the North London Polytechnic in the late 1980s (Women for Science for Women, 1987). The Edinburgh Women's Science Forum was set up in 1986 to bring together women working in academia and industry with lay women who were interested in learning about science. Its main activity was producing exhibitions for the Edinburgh Science Festival (Women for Science for Women, 1987). In 1987 Equal Bytes was set up as a support group for women learning and teaching computing at all levels (Women into Computing, 1988, pp79-81).

From the late 1990s networking groups were developed, perhaps due to the expansion of the internet and the resurgence of government and corporate interest in women's participation in SECT. In 1999 Sandi Rhys-Jones and Cheryl Rendell of Rhys-Jones Consultants launched a communications network entitled Change the Face of Construction. This tapped into the developing agenda around corporate diversity and aimed to facilitate the participation of women and ethnic minorities in the construction industry. Unusually, the activities of this network targeted employers as well as women working in construction. Its website disseminated best practice on gender equality, and Rhys-Jones and Rendell provided practical help and consultancy to employers which included gathering statistics, collating examples of good practice and sources of expertise and liaising with the media. On a larger scale the consultants delivered equal opportunities training within companies, taught careers and personal development courses, supplied speakers for events and carried out equal opportunities audits (Change the Face of Construction, 2007).

South West Women in Construction (SWWIC) was set up in the early 2000s to support women in all areas of the industry (South West Women in Construction, 2006). Chicks with Bricks was created in 2005 by women architects Pascale Scheurer and Holly Porter with the support of Women in Architecture and the National Association of Women in Construction (Chicks with Bricks, 2007). In the field of science the Women's Industrial Network in Pharmaceuticals (WIN in Pharma) operated briefly in the early 2000s to help women progress in the pharmaceuticals industry (Association for Women in Science and Engineering, 2001b). In the mid-2000s, Mums in Science was set up as a web-based forum and portal to help women scientists with children achieve work/life balance. It was sponsored by EuroSciCon, a European organisation which organised scientific conferences and meetings (Mums in Science, 2007).

Many informal networks for women in SECT were focused on the IT and communications sector, perhaps because women in these professions were familiar with web-based communications tools. American venture capitalist Lucy Marcus founded HighTech Women in London in 2000 and by the mid-2000s it had almost 2000 registered members and 6000 regular visitors to its website. Its sub-project Skills Bank for Society was launched in 2001 as an opportunity for members to donate their skills to non-profit organisations (HighTech Women, 2004; personal correspondence). Women in Telecoms and Technology was founded in 2001 by four senior women in the industry: Stephanie Liston, Annette Nabavi, Sue McDougall, and Anne Heal. By the mid-2000s membership had grown via word of mouth to over 400 (Women in Telecoms and Technology, 2007). The Digital Women's Network was set up in the early 2000s for women working in digital media in the north east (Digital Women's Network, 2006).

Untold, a network for female digital designers, began in 2002 with an exhibition of women's work which was curated by designer Jane Austin at the Institute of Contemporary Arts. But financial resources were scarce from the outset and the network had dissolved by 2007 (Pitt, 2003b). In 2005 a web-based network and information portal entitled Womenintechnology was set up by Maggie Berry of McGregor Boyal Associates, a financial services recruitment firm. Between 2005 and 2007 the website was regularly used by about 9000 female IT professionals and had built up an active network of over 2000 individuals who were committed to promoting women's participation in technology. In 2006 Womenintechnology sponsored an award at the BlackBerry Women and Technology Awards and a new category at the European Banking Technology Awards (Womenintechnology, 2007; personal correspondence). There were also many international groups such as Systers and Women in Technology International which had a substantial British membership.

4. Women's groups within professional associations

Women's groups within SECT professional associations worked for the participation and advancement of women from inside the scientific and industrial establishment. They did this through facilitating networking for women members of professional associations, producing newsletters and websites to support women and raise their profile within the associations and surveying women members to establish their needs. This provided a basis for the groups to produce reports and lobby the professional associations on the needs of their women members and the issue of women's participation in SECT. These groups often organised events and conferences and engaged in outreach at schools and universities. One of the earliest was the Women in Physics Committee of the Institute of Physics, created in 1985 to advise the Institute on gender issues (Science Policy Support Group, 1992b). The Institute of Physics Women in Physics Group was set up in 1995, with a brief to encourage women to participate in Institute activities and to support them in their professional development (Women in Physics Group, 2004).

The Royal Astronomical Society Committee for Women in Astronomy and Geophysics was set up in 1989 in response to an open letter to the Society written by 25 female astronomers and countersigned by a further 216 astronomers and geophysicists. Yvonne Elsworth chaired the initial committee, which conducted a survey of Royal Astronomical Society members and other female astronomers. Its survey report, published in 1995, advised that the Society should invite women speakers to meetings, ensure that its image reflected the diversity of its membership, provide crèche facilities for meetings and disseminate careers advice and help to female astronomers (Walker, 2002). In 1996 the Committee for Women in Astronomy and Geophysics became a standing committee of the Society with a brief to represent female members and young female astronomers (Walker, 2006).

The Women Members' Network of the Royal Society of Chemistry was founded in 1991 as a collection of ten regionally based, self-organised groups for women members of the Society. It was engaged in promoting the Rosalind Franklin Award (see Chapter Six) and assisting with the development of the Association for Women in Science and Engineering. The Society also developed a relationship with the Daphne Jackson Trust: all Daphne Jackson fellows were given free Society membership for the duration of their fellowship. Other links were made with the Athena project, the UK Resource Centre for Women in SET and the Women's National Commission. In 2003 the Society launched a report on the recruitment and retention of women in academic chemistry which was co-ordinated by a working party chaired by Professor Dame Julia Higgins. By the mid-2000s there were only a few women's groups within the Society but links continued with other women's organisations (Royal Society of Chemistry, 2007; personal correspondence).

In 2001 software engineer Sue Black set up BCSWomen, the women's group of the British Computer Society (BCS). This web-based group provided networking opportunities and support to both female BCS members and other women working in IT around the world and in its first five years registered 500 members (BCSWomen, 2007; personal communication). The Women in IT Working Group (WITWG), set up in 2004 to report on gender issues to the BCS Board of Trustees, was the catalyst for the development of a BCS Women's Forum which worked with employers and other women's groups (British Computer Society, 2007). In 2002 the Women in Plumbing Group at the Institute of Plumbing and Heating Engineering was set up partly in response to a growing customer demand for female plumbers, and skills shortages in the industry which had created a strong business case for gender equality.

As well as the usual activities, the group arranged visits to manufac-
turers and training days to update women on new products (Women in
Plumbing Group, 2006).

Women's groups in SECT professional associations were particularly
important because professional associations had historically policed
the boundaries of certain occupations in order to keep women out
(Witz, 1992). These groups may have been in a better position to change
sexist attitudes and masculine cultures within the professions than
groups outside SECT. Significantly however, many professional associations in SECT, particularly in the construction industry, did not have
women's groups or many female members (Bennett, Davidson and
Gale, 1999). Also notably, Lady Susan Greenfield, Director of the Royal
Institution and arguably Britain's most famous female contemporary
scientist, was repeatedly rejected as a fellow of the Royal Society,
Britain's oldest scientific institution (Adam, 2005). By 2007 only 5 per
cent of the fellowship of the Royal Society was female, even though increasing proportions of women had been elected in the 2000s (Royal
Society, 2007) and although the Society housed the Athena project on
gender equality (see Chapter Six) there was still no dedicated group to
support its women fellows.

5. Groups in universities

Between the 1980s and mid-2000s many universities developed general
gender equality initiatives and groups were set up for women
academics and students in SECT to encourage students into SECT disciplines. These provided networking, mentoring and support for existing women faculty and students, worked to make the SECT curriculum
more relevant to women and attempted to improve the university
environment for women students and academics. Groups organised
events such as academic seminars and skills development workshops
for women, and set up websites and produced newsletters for their
membership. They conducted research and produced reports on the
issue of women in SECT and good gender equality practice, developed
print and multimedia curriculum materials with the interests of women
in mind, advised course development panels and lobbied university
departments and management on gender issues. Some women only
courses were set up at universities and colleges, and taster days were

organised for schoolgirls. The groups tried to help women who had taken career breaks return to work and sometimes gave small grants to women who could not obtain departmental funding for conferences and workshops.

In the early 1980s Susan Bullivant, an engineer at Loughborough University, encouraged the students in her department to form a group for mutual support and school outreach (Raat, Harding, and Mottier, 1981a). In 1984 the Open University (OU) Women into Science and Engineering (WISE) Working Group was set up, chaired by Ruth Carter and Gill Kirkup. WISE supported the development of the Technology Women's Information Network and was instrumental in increasing the representation of women on the university's Technology Foundation course from 18 per cent in 1979 to 29 per cent in 1989. Together with the OU Women in Technology project, it was the recipient of a Fawcett Society Award. The OU also housed a Women Into Computing group and equal opportunities groups in the faculties of Technology, Science, and Mathematics (Carter and Kirkup, 1991; personal correspondence).

Between 1989 and 1991 Maggie Woodrow and Ann Bridgwood developed and delivered the Women in Science and Technology (WIST) project at the Polytechnic of North London, funded by the Department of Employment. It incorporated a research programme around the reasons for women's under-representation in SECT subjects and a number of practical strategies. The Higher Introductory Technological Education Conversion Course had one stream targeted at women with childcare responsibilities, and access and foundation courses with a high proportion of women students were established at several further education colleges. A taster course was developed for fourth and fifth form pupils interested in SECT higher education, in an effort to recruit girls. Bridgwood produced a handbook detailing strategies for staff working with women science and technology students in further and higher education (Bridgwood, 1991).

In 1985 the Women into Technology and Science (WITS) access course commenced at Huddersfield Polytechnic. It aimed to empower working-class and unqualified women by giving them opportunities to pursue non-traditional subjects in higher education. Twenty four participants were recruited each year to study subjects including maths, physics, computing, materials science, electronics and biochemistry. The teaching methods included open learning, group work, library research, practicals, laboratory work, oral presentations and constructing artefacts and the focus was on building confidence and personal skills such as relaxation and stress management. The schedule was full-time, and the teaching timetabled during the school day. Women who had toddlers could use the nursery at the Polytechnic or receive an allowance for childcare. All students received a training allowance from the Local Authority. Many WITS participants progressed into higher education: the course was still operating in the mid 2000s and was heavily oversubscribed (Gibbs and Thompson, 1992; personal correspondence).

In 1993 the University of Cambridge joined the Opportunity 2000 campaign (see Chapter Six) and set up a Women in Science committee to investigate how to improve the participation of women in SECT at the university. In 1999 Nancy Lane of the Department of Zoology and Felicity Hunt, Head of Equality and Diversity, established the Women in Science, Engineering and Technology Initiative (WiSETI). This was funded by and operated under the aegis of the Personnel division, with additional financial support from the Colleges and the University's learning and teaching budget (University of Cambridge, 2006). It was launched at the Cambridge University computer laboratory in the early 2000s to support women engaged in computing research. It was supported by organisations and institutions that included Microsoft Research, Intel Cambridge Research, Newnham College, Queen Mary University of London, the Cambridge-MIT Institute, and the Oxford Internet Institute (Women @ CL, 2005-2007).

In 1995 the Higher Education Funding Council in Scotland set aside £300,000 for the WISET initiative which focused on improving the recruitment, retention and progression of women in SECT. This sought to facilitate the development, dissemination and adoption of good practice in all Scottish higher education institutions. WISET initially conducted research and published several good practice guides in 1997 which were disseminated throughout the sector. At the same time, seven institutional projects for women in SECT were established incorporating aspects of this good practice. These included the Girls Get SET project at Heriot-Watt University, a postgraduate mentoring scheme at Edinburgh University and an inclusive teaching project at St Andrews. From 1997 on the Council made an annual commitment of £100,000 for the Winning Women project, a collaborative partnership between several institutions which produced a number of texts around good practice. An advisory group was set up, chaired by Ann Kettle, to oversee the initiative. Between 1999 and 2003 a national co-ordinator was appointed to manage women in SECT activities, liaising with contacts and representatives in every Scottish Higher Education Institution. Rosa Michaelson, the first co-ordinator, also set up links with the Athena Project, AWiSE and Women into Computing, and contributed to the 2002 Greenfield Report on women in SECT (personal correspondence).

Loughborough University conducted a gender audit in the 1990s and instigated an equal pay policy, a career breaks scheme, a campus nursery, childcare vouchers, a flexi-time system, parental leave and vacation playschemes for children. In partnership with Nottingham University, Loughborough was awarded a grant from the Athena project in 1999 to set up a programme of workshops and mentoring for women with up to five years of postdoctoral experience in SECT. The following year an East Midlands network for women in SECT was set up in a partnership between Loughborough and the universities of De Montfort, Leicester, Nottingham and Nottingham Trent. Loughborough was the site for a number of research projects around gender and SECT, disseminating information and good practice via its website and a major conference. In 2003 it won the Equality Challenge Unit (ECU) prize in the Royal Society Athena Awards for its gender equality work (Royal Society, 2006).

In the early 2000s the Athena project Scientific Women's Academic Network (SWAN) was set up in partnership with London Metropolitan University. This virtual network provided web-based recourses, guidance and information for new universities in the south east to raise the profile of women in SECT within these institutions. Universities signing up to the Athena SWAN charter established in 2005 were asked to commit to tackling the unequal representation of women in science by examining and overcoming structural and personal obstacles by changing cultures and attitudes. The prevalence of short-term contract working which had especially negative consequences for the retention and progression of women was a central concern. By 2006 the charter had been signed by 23 universities and Athena gave awards to Sunderland, Bristol, Cambridge, University College London, Edinburgh, Nottingham, Oxford, Plymouth, and Southampton, among others. University College London had set up a SWAN Senior Advisory Group of academics to advise on and monitor initiatives and to promote the charter throughout the sector (Royal Society, 2006; personal communication).

Many university initiatives around women in SECT took place during the early 2000s, several with the support of Athena. ResNET was launched in 2000 at the University of East Anglia as a support network for women contract research staff in the science schools and at the Norwich Research Park (Association for Women in Science and Engineering, 2001a; ResNET, 2007). Measures undertaken at the University of Bristol included a women returners' scheme for academics within the faculties of Engineering, Science and Medical and Veterinary Sciences which provided up to six months protected research time for women returning from maternity leave (Royal Society, 2006). At the University of Plymouth, the Women in Technology Network (WITNET) was set up under the leadership of Liz Hodgkinson and funded by the UK Resource Centre for Women in Science, Engineering and Technology (WITNET, 2007).

The Esslemont Group, a women's network within the College of Life Sciences and Medicine at the University of Aberdeen, was formed in 2002 after the publication of the Greenfield report and a one day symposium entitled Women on Top: Reflections of Women in Science. This was focused on the benefits women could bring to scientific education and employment and how to promote their participation. The group was named after the first female graduate from the Faculty, Mary Esslemont, and became affiliated to the Association of Women in Science and Engineering in March 2003 (Esslemont Group, 2007). In 2005, Women in Science, Engineering, and Technology (WiSET) was set up at the University of Manchester as a network for women students and staff in the Faculty of Engineering and Physical Science (WiSET, 2006).

6. Courses for women returners

In the debate around women's career potential in SECT, women returners were often identified as a valuable and under-used human
resource. Official discussion reached its peak with the 2002 DTI-com-
missioned report *Maximising Returns*, which found that only 25 per
cent of female science, engineering and technology graduates were employed in relevant occupations and argued that tapping this lost talent
would help to fill skills shortages (People Science and Policy Ltd, 2002,
p6). It reported that women who attempted to return to work in science,
engineering and technology had more difficulty than women returning
to other occupations, because of their belief that their skills were out of
date and the inflexibility of the working arrangements in these sectors
(People Science and Policy Ltd, 2002, pp68-69). However, these issues
were not new: when *Maximising Returns* was launched a variety of projects specifically targeted at women returners had been in place for
almost twenty years which were run by individuals, groups, companies,
government agencies and educational and other institutions. These
largely took the form of grants and/or courses enabling women returners to update their skills and rebuild their confidence.

The Daphne Jackson Trust, one of the first major schemes for women
returners to SECT, was set up in 1985 by Professor Daphne Jackson of
the University of Surrey, the first woman professor of physics in Britain.
The scheme funded flexible and part-time fellowships, tenable within
university departments, which were intended to provide opportunities
for qualified women to rebuild their expertise and self-confidence and
eventually return to permanent academic posts. The scheme operated
with industry sponsorship: the first group of fellows were funded by
British Gas, British Telecom, GEC, the Leverhulme Trust and the Institute of Physics (Jackson, 1985). After Professor Jackson's death in 1991
the scheme continued, and achieved registered charity status in 1992.
As well as funding the fellowships the Trust organised events such as
networking receptions and skills development seminars and produced
literature and other materials to raise awareness of the issue of women
in SECT. In the early 2000s it developed an Industrial Associates Placement Scheme with the Equalitec project (see Chapter Six), which provided one year placements in industry. By the mid-2000s the Trust was
receiving almost 250 enquiries per year and had awarded 145 fellow-

ships in total. Evaluation suggested that it had been successful in building skills and confidence and in enabling over 70 per cent of its fellows to return to high level careers (Daphne Jackson Trust, 2007; personal communication).

Just after the Daphne Jackson Trust was set up, government and industry bodies also began to support women returners. The Training Agency sponsored a series of Masters level courses entitled *Women into Industry* which were targeted at women with first degrees in science and engineering subjects. The aim was for participants to return to work, further their careers and perhaps enter senior management (Holton, 1989). The employers' association Women into IT set up a Returner Working Party which explored ways of helping employers to attract and retain women returners (Women into IT, 1990a). Companies such as British Aerospace, British Telecom, IBM, and the Inland Revenue were represented at seminars which were designed to raise awareness of issues for women returners and to discuss possible solutions (Women into IT, 1990b). Schemes were put in place in individual companies: International Computers Limited ran a course entitled WISE UP (Women in Software Engineering Update) aimed at women with experience of systems development or programming (Women into IT, 1990a).

Universities and colleges developed courses for women returners as part of wider gender equality initiatives. In the late 1980s Lancaster and Morecambe Continuing Education Centre launched a 28-week course entitled WIST (Women into Science and Technology) which was designed to help women returners to the emergent field of new technology (Women into Computing, 1988, p9). As part of the JIVE project (see Chapter Five) in the 2000s, Sheffield Hallam University delivered a course for women returners in the built environment sector, running for three days a week over a period of five months. A work placement was included and childcare and travel costs were paid (UK Resource Centre for Women in SET, 2006b). JIVE and the Scottish Resource Centre for Women in Science, Engineering, and Technology sponsored a series of free Saturday workshops for women returners to the fields of life sciences and electronics, incorporating job shadowing and a free on-site crèche (Sheffield Hallam University, 2006). The Queen Mary University of London Departments of Computer Science and Electronic

Engineering were awarded ESF grants to enable women who were on a career break or unemployed to participate in MSc courses in Bioinformatics, Internet Computing, e-Commerce Engineering, Information Management, and Intelligent Web Technologies (Queen Mary University of London, 2006).

Case Study 4.2: Women Returners at the Open University
The Open University Women in Technology project was set up in 1982 by Ailsa Swarbrick of the OU and Geoff Chivers of Loughborough University, with funding from the Manpower Services Commission and support from the Engineering Industry Training Board and the Women's Engineering Society. Initially it aimed to enable women with previous qualifications and experience in engineering and technology to return to work, but the scheme expanded in 1984 to include training for women with no previous technological qualifications. Trainees were enrolled on a relevant Open University course, offered vocational and educational counselling and training in job seeking and interviews, and given the chance of work placements. The training incorporated an element of confidence building and sought to help trainees acquire a group identity and develop solidarity as women. The all-female project team provided telephone advice and support. Course fees and travelling expenses were covered for all students (Swarbrick and Atkins, 1991; personal correspondence).

By 1992 three schemes were in operation: Women Returners to Information Technology, Electronics, and Computing (WRITE) which offered courses including programming, IT, databases, software engineering, computational mathematics and electronics; Women Returners to Environmental Management and Control (WREN), which offered courses including environmental control, monitoring, ecology, oceanography, sedimentation and basin analysis and systems management; and Women Returners to Industrial Processing and Manufacturing (WRIP), which offered courses including control engineering, instrumentation, computer-aided design and industrial materials (SPSG, 1992a). Over 600 women accessed this project during its first ten years (Swarbrick and Atkins, 1991, p7) and the proportion who obtained employment began at 80 per cent and steadily improved (Swarbrick and Atkins, 1991, p8). However, there were barriers to employment such as the lack of flexible working arrangements, difficulties arranging childcare and the broader context of economic recession, and disabled and ethnic minority women found it difficult to take part (Swarbrick *et al*, 1990 and 1993).

In response to the *Maximising Returns* and *SET Fair* reports in the early 2000s (see also Chapter Six), Clem Herman developed a course at the Open University for women returners, coded T160. This university level module, sponsored by the Department of Trade and Industry and the ESF through the UK Resource Centre for Women in SET and based largely online, was designed to reach women with qualifications in science, engineering and technology, including those who were geographically isolated. Teaching was delivered through interactive online lectures and discussions that helped women analyse their previous work experience, identify possible job opportunities and develop an action plan to find employment. Course content, developed by a team from the Open University and the UKRC, focused on the development of skills and confidence. Students were offered mentoring and networking opportunities with potential employers and role models. No fees were required, and childcare and travel expenses were provided when necessary (Open University, 2006; personal correspondence). By 2007 the course had registered over 700 women in four cohorts and informal evaluation suggested that it had helped many of them to increase their confidence and define new career aspirations. To sustain the course, it was adapted to become a mainstream Open University module for both female and male returners, delivered entirely online through the university's Virtual Learning Environment platform (UK Resource Centre for Women in SET, 2006a, pp12-13; personal correspondence).

7. Discussion

The co-construction of gender and SECT begins in education and continues throughout the career trajectory. In the period covered by this study, the workplace took on particular importance in the reproduction of and struggle over gender relations as increasing numbers of middle-class women entered the arena of paid work and became breadwinners in their own right (Bradley, 1999, p210). But although women's position in higher education and the professions showed a gradual improvement, the segregation of disciplines and occupational sectors persisted. Women were still over-represented in subjects such as arts and languages and among workers in service sectors, education and health, and still under-represented in the physical sciences and engineering, technology, computing and construction. Segregation in the professions endured, although women made inroads into SECT subjects at school and university, a process termed the 'leaky pipeline' (Osborn *et al*, 2000). Table 4.3 shows that in 2000/01 women dominated areas of the curriculum such as psychology, education, medicine, languages, humanities and creative arts and design at postgraduate as well as undergraduate levels. However, attrition at postgraduate levels meant that subjects such as physics, computing science, engineering, and architecture, building and planning were heavily male dominated, despite over thirty years of gender equality initiatives.

Table 4.3 Qualifications attained on higher education courses by level and subject area 2000/01

Subject	Undergraduate % Women	Postgraduate % Women
Psychology	82	76
Education	77	72
Medicine, Dentistry, and allied subjects	74	66
Languages, Humanities, Creative Arts & Design	64	59
Biology	61	50
Social, economic & political studies	61	56
Law and Business and Administrative Studies	56	48
Chemistry	43	36
Mathematical Sciences	41	36
Architecture, Building and Planning	26	36
Computing Science	22	31
Physics	20	22
Engineering	13	17

(Promoting SET for Women Unit, 2003)

By the early 2000s women constituted 45 per cent of the total labour force: Table 4.4 shows that women made up the majority of employees in service sectors, health and social work and education, and were a minority in sectors such as manufacturing, transport, storage and communication, agriculture and fishing, energy and water and construction. Women working in such male-dominated sectors were mainly employed in clerical and secretarial positions while the men in traditionally female-dominated sectors dominated management positions (Promoting SET for Women Unit, 2003). Women with dependent children were the least likely group in the labour market to be employed and in the group of women with dependent children over the age of five, women with SECT degrees were considerably less likely to be employed than their counterparts with non-SECT degrees (People Science and Policy Ltd, 2002, p9). Women with SECT degrees were economically less active than their male counterparts across the board (People Science and Policy Ltd, 2002, p68).

Table 4.4 Employment by major sector by sex 2001

Sector	% Women
Health and social work	80
Education	72
Hotels and restaurants	58
Banking, insurance and pension funding	52
Other services	52
Wholesale, retail and motor trade	50
Public administration and defence	47
Real estate, renting and business	41
Manufacturing	25
Transport, storage and communication	25
Agriculture and fishing	21
Energy and water	20
Construction	9

(Promoting SET for Women Unit, 2003)

By the early 2000s British universities were still among the worst institutions in the country in terms of gender equity, often paying lip service to equal opportunities but showing no substantive action (Saunderson, 2002, p377; Bagilhole and Goode, 2001, p163). Table 4.5 shows the situation in the academic employment sector in 2000 when, despite the increased proportion of female undergraduate and postgraduate students in many fields, women were poorly represented even at junior lecturing levels, particularly in mathematics, physical sciences and technology. The highest percentage of women among junior lecturing staff was 56 per cent in medicine, dentistry and health, but they constituted only 18 per cent of the professors in this field. Only 2 per cent of mathematics professors, 4 per cent of chemistry professors, and 3 per cent of professors in engineering and technology and physics were women.

Table 4.5 Full-time junior lecturers and professors in UK universities 2000/01

Discipline area	Junior lecturers % Women	Professors % Women
Medicine, dentistry, health	56	18
Languages	52	21
Education	52	26
Administration, business, social studies	37	14
Humanities and arts	36	15
Biosciences	30	9
IT, systems sciences	28	14
Architecture, built environment, planning	21	8
Mathematics	19	2
Chemistry	16	4
Engineering & technology	15	3
Physics	9	3

(Promoting SET for Women Unit, 2003)

The initiatives and groups described in this chapter undoubtedly had significant impact in helping women to cope with male-dominated SECT workplaces. And some groups did critique and try to reform masculine workplace cultures. However, in order to achieve substantive gender equality in SECT a stronger challenge to institutions would be required, rather than merely supporting women through supplementary or semi-independent initiatives. As well as strong critical engagement with SECT cultures, structural inequalities such as the gender pay gap and the lack of family-friendly facilities and issues such as sexual harassment have to be addressed. Such an approach would link with broader feminist positions about the organisation of public and private life and state and corporate responsibility for the reproductive sphere (see also Chapter Six), demands for both paid and unpaid work to be recognised as essential societal contributions, and the idea that men should contribute more fully to domestic life (Lister, 2002; Acker, 2004). Without such changes, women's increased participation in any professional sector could not achieve gender equality and would be likely to perpetuate the exploitation of working-class and immigrant women who have historically taken on the caring responsibilities of Western middle-class professionals (Acker, 2004).

It is vital to understand how systemic gendered hierarchies have been reproduced through the definition of the professional and the structures of the labour market. From a feminist perspective labour market segregation is neither coincidental nor a reflection of natural gender differences but the result of a system which sorts men and women into different employment sectors and ensures that those which are male-dominated carry social status and greater economic rewards. The labour market, like the family, is a key institution in which patriarchal power is institutionalised. The patriarchal system is partly maintained by restricting women's access to professions which could give them economic and social power, to encourage them to marry and to maintain their dependence on their husbands. Different types of labour market segregation are implicated in this process: horizontal segregation ensures that women are concentrated in lower paying and lower status areas of the labour market, while vertical segregation ensures that within all labour market sectors men continue to conserve most of the wealth and can control women at work as they do at home (Witz, 1992; Bradley, 1999).

Women's access to certain professions has historically been restricted by denying them educational opportunities, the masculinisation of professional institutions and the definition of the category of the professional. Patriarchal power has defined women as unable to exercise important forms of knowledge which are the basis for high-status professions. Thus the construction of SECT knowledge and the masculine SECT professional has been an important strategy for occupational closure. Awarding of credentials for SECT professions has rated masculine skills as more important, and women have been denied access to acquiring these skills while feminine skills have at the same time been devalued (Witz, 1992; Bradley, 1999; Bagilhole and Goode, 2001). Women's scientific discoveries have been overlooked or attributed to their male colleagues, Rosalind Franklin being an especially high-profile case (Bebbington, 2002, p366). The cultural masculinity of SECT professions has functioned to maintain men's dominance and to exclude women or to control and restrict those within SECT sectors (Bagilhole and Goode, 2001). Female-dominated occupations such as nursing and social work have historically been associated with a different skill-set and a submission to male authority and are defined as semi-professions (Witz, 1992, p60).

Because of this gendered hierarchy of professions male ownership of SECT is institutionalised at a fundamental level, even when women are a sizeable minority (Ellis, 2003, p10). As a result, many women who achieve senior roles in SECT become part of the patriarchal project by taking on masculine values and practices, and do little to work towards gender equality (Bown, 1999, p7). Male ownership of SECT means that equal gender representation would not necessarily transform cultures and practices, without an engagement with the concept of power relations and the purposes served by the chilly climate. Women may just become co-opted into masculine institutions, or SECT professions with an equal gender representation may become feminised and lose status, like the medical profession (Jones, 2004).

Various groups for women professionals in SECT have made demands, but have failed to combine them into a common political platform and strong collective engagement with SECT institutions. However, when assessing the activities of these groups it is important to understand the difficulty of critiquing and changing SECT, particularly from within.

Activist work has been structured and in many cases constrained by various factors including the backlash against feminism, the prevalence of the business case approach to gender equality (see Chapter Six), and the fact that many activists are SECT professionals who are situated within the very cultures and institutions they must challenge. Because of these interlocking factors, putting in place critical and transformative initiatives around women's participation in SECT has been politically, professionally and personally dangerous (Phipps, 2006).

Support and networking groups for women in SECT have performed valuable functions, as evidenced by the growing number of these groups and the increasing number of women involved. It is crucial that such groups begin to deconstruct the patriarchal systems which deny women power, knowledge and money by excluding them from or restricting them within male-dominated professions and defining female-dominated professions as inferior. Arguing for equal opportunities without tackling these deeper factors could be seen, as Wendy Saunderson says, as putting 'lipstick on the gorilla' (Saunderson, 2002, p376).

5

Masculine skills and women's empowerment
Training women in the trades and ICTs

Chapter Four looked at groups which supported women in SECT professions, and this chapter centres on women's training and employment in manual trades and at technician level and considers general technology literacy. The discussion is divided into two parts: the first focuses on the issue of women in manual trades and the second on women and information and communication technologies (ICTs). The construction industry has historically been the most male-dominated sector of the UK economy and women have been concentrated in lower paid and non-technical positions such as clerical work and human resources rather than skilled technical and trades occupations (Pillbeam and Farren, 2004, p10). Women were a small minority of ICT technicians when these technologies spread into common usage in the 1990s and were identified as in need of support with general ICT literacy. Initiatives designed to tackle these issues were based at further education colleges and dedicated women's centres rather than at schools and universities and underpinned by frameworks around social exclusion and a more explicit feminist politics than initiatives aimed at girls and female SECT professionals. Women-only training courses led by supportive female tutors have been the main format of delivery, targeted at groups such as ethnic minority women, lone mothers, disabled women and women from disadvantaged areas. This chapter examines a number of such initiatives.

1. Women's participation in manual trades

Participation in skills-based training and skilled trades has been more gendered than any other area of education and work although the trades and skills considered masculine and feminine have varied through time (Cockburn, 1983 and 1985; Bennett, Davidson and Gale, 1999). During the two World Wars thousands of women retrained to fill the skilled manual jobs in engineering and construction which were left vacant by men (Gurjao, 2006, p16), but in the post-war period trades unions colluded with employers and the state in driving these women back out of the sector (Clarke *et al*, 2005, p153). Table 5.1 opposite shows that in the building trades women's participation between the 1930s and the 1970s failed to rise above 1 per cent, despite the intervening war.

By the 1970s women were still only a small minority of workers in the construction industry and most were employed in administrative and associate functions, while few worked in the skilled manual trades (Clarke *et al*, 2005, p154). Women's employment declined during the 1980s because of the diminishing functions of the Direct Labour Organisations and the growth of self-employment and competitive tendering, plus general economic recession (Blackwell, 1992, p14). Of the 9,107 electrical contracting apprentices being trained in England and Scotland in 1983, only nine were women. In 1985 women were almost 10 per cent of construction workers in Greater London but less than 1 per cent were employed in craft, technician and managerial jobs (Women in Construction Advisory Group, 1985, p2).

Official discussion of the issue of women's vocational training began in the mid-1970s, a little before the 1975 Sex Discrimination Act. The Training Agency reported that although women were beginning to break into non-traditional courses, there was a need for pilot courses for girls, support for careers officers, training at junior levels, training for mature women and flexible career structures (Training Services Agency 1975, pp26-27). The Sex Discrimination Act was the lever for women to access Training Opportunity Programme (TOPS) courses, which allowed them to acquire craft skills outside the apprenticeship system, although there were still problems with indirect discrimination (Women and Manual Trades, 1981 and 1984; Clarke and Wall, 2004). The Manpower Services Commission provided sponsorship for participants

Table 5.1 Gender breakdown in a variety of skilled trades 1931-1971

Occupational Division		1931	1951	1961	1971
Carpenters and Joiners	Women	49	716	1,060	920
	Men	246,807	244,213	260.240	293,200
Bricklayers	Women	775	153	No figures	160
	Men	692,123	141,699	available	1,1433,140
Labourers	Women	139	607	750	1620
	Men	172,352	288,899	243,410	1,433,140
Painters and Decorators	Women	2,564	10,388	11,920	5,180
	Men	203,759	298,566	294,400	235,870
Total in all Building Trades	Women	3,527	12,494	14,230	9,330
	Men	1,315,041	1,672,153	1,311,800	1,346,010
Women as % of building workforce		0.3%	0.74%	1%	0.7%

(Clarke and Wall, 2004, p35)

in Wider Opportunities for Women (WOW) courses running at several colleges and universities, which included job sampling and careers counselling (Further Education Unit, 1981, p18, p20). When the Training Agency took over from the Manpower Services Commission in the late 1980s it continued this work through five Focus on Women projects which offered information on education and training opportunities (Business in the Community, 1989, p19).

In 1979 and 1980 the Further Education Unit responded to the issue of women's training through the reports *A Basis for Choice* and *Further Opportunities in Focus*. These led to *Balancing the Equation* (1981), suggesting how staff at FE colleges could improve women's participation in non-traditional training. Its recommendations, put in place in several London colleges, included using women staff as role models, offering taster courses, providing extra tutoring and support, and raising staff awareness of different learning needs. But it was considered to be too radical to institute women only courses (Further Education Unit, 1981, pp5-6). The Women's National Commission report *The Other Half of Our Future* (1984) made additional recommendations for educationalists (Further Education Unit, 1985, pp18-19). A 1985 Further Education Unit policy statement then recommended developing a more learner-centred curriculum, avoiding timetabling which prevented non-traditional choices, making guidance staff aware of equal opportunities, allowing flexible learning to meet the needs of women with caring commitments and accrediting prior learning experiences. It was suggested that women only courses should be set up and that women's studies modules should be instituted for the purpose of consciousness raising (Further Education Unit, 1985, pp9-11).

Some local authorities made efforts to improve the representation of tradeswomen in the Direct Labour Organisations (DLOs) which delivered construction and building maintenance in local areas in the 1980s. Haringey Council in North London set up a new-build site where the majority of workers and the site agent were women (Clarke and Wall, 2004). Similarly, Hackney Council in East London adopted an equal opportunities policy and set up an adult training scheme in the trades which was partly intended to be a positive action initiative. By 1985 ten of the fifteen participants were women and a more advanced training course was set up with more than half the ten places per year taken by women. A grant from the European Social Fund enabled the scheme to provide childcare. However, by the late 1980s the Council faced problems with funding and cutbacks to its own building projects which were a source of potential employment for trainees (Eclipse Publications, 1990, p21). In general, Thatcherite centralisation of government had a devastating effect on the DLOs and by the mid-1990s their functions had been reduced mostly to maintenance, new build work having been privatised (Clarke and Wall, 2004). Nevertheless, some councils continued to support tradeswomen into the 1990s through Local Labour in Construction schemes (Women and Manual Trades, 1995).

In the wider employment sector, 1982 saw the launch of a Union of Construction, Allied Trades and Technicians (UCATT) working party on the employment of women (Eclipse Publications, 1990, p17). In 1984 the Women in Construction Advisory Group was created, incorporating employers, trades unions, policy-makers and training providers under the leadership of the Greater London Council (Women in Construction Advisory Group, 1985). By the late 1980s the problem of skills shortages in construction had led to interest from industry bodies: in 1989 the Building Employers' Confederation reported that 51 per cent of firms suffered from shortages of bricklayers, 51 per cent from shortages of carpenters and 40 per cent from shortages of plasterers. It set up a working party on recruitment which considered the recruitment of women. By 1994 the Latham Report and ensuing Construction Industry Board working group report reflected the emergence of a strong business case for promoting women's participation in manual trades (Dainty, Bagilhole and Neale, 2001, p297). All these developments provided the context for the initiatives described in this chapter, many of which incorporated a strategic use of the business case for women's training and used private sector sponsorship and central and local government money to match their European grants.

a. Women only training

The challenge to the content of girls' and women's education, and the emphasis placed in adult education on parenting and domestic skills, were major components of both first and second wave women's movements. The second wave incorporated a campaign for broadening the curriculum and developing women only courses as safe contexts for acquiring skills and building confidence. In 1981 the first women's education centre opened in Southampton funded by Southampton University, the local education authority, the Workers' Educational Association and the Equal Opportunities Commission. Various forms of provision followed, including courses for women returners, courses in non-traditional skills and women's studies courses. Access courses, providing a route to university for those without the required qualifications, were launched during the 1970s and 1980s and attracted a large proportion of women (Benn, 1998, p44). By the 1990s a range of educational initiatives for women were offered by colleges, universities, local authorities, the Workers' Educational Association, women's training centres and other voluntary organisations and financed by the European Social Fund, the Further Education Funding Council, the Training and Enterprise Councils, and local economic development and regeneration budgets (McGivney, 1998, p9).

Women only training courses in non-traditional skills were an important element of this provision, and blended feminist politics with the policy concerns emerging around women in masculine professions (Faulkner, 2004). Training in women only groups was largely delivered by supportive female tutors. It focused on developing confidence as well as skills and incorporated an element of consciousness raising around gender inequality. Workshops were offered in trades such as electronics, carpentry, joinery, motor mechanics, plastering, bricklaying, painting and decorating and plumbing. ICT training was often part of the package, particularly in later initiatives. Priority was given to those who had difficulty in accessing training such as ethnic minority women, women with disabilities, lone mothers and women without qualifications and financial help was often given in the form of fee waivers and travel expenses. Students were often provided with a crèche or help with childcare costs and courses were mainly run in school hours and during the school term. Such courses were underpinned by ideas about challenging patriarchal constructions of femininity, empowering women through giving them economic independence and helping them to influence and shape the built environment around them. Students were generally women whose career trajectories would otherwise have led to low paid service sector jobs which had connotations about feminine appearance and behaviour and subservience to male management. Having practical skills was also seen as a way for women to escape dependence on their husbands.

The framework of women only training drew heavily on the ideas and politics of the women's liberation movement and many tutors and students were themselves active in feminist politics and set up workers' co-operatives built on the concept of communal living. However, to facilitate women's progression into further training or employment educators had to co-operate with the mainstream (Women and Manual Trades, 1978) and this created tension. In addition, radical feminists in the movement were concerned that tradeswomen were imitating patriarchal behaviour and feared that becoming 'one of the lads' was a form of co-option. Questions were over the long-term implications of introducing women into masculine fields without challenging the gender segregation of the labour market itself (Women and Manual Trades, 1978 and 1983). There were further conflicts around sexuality: lesbians were well represented among tradeswomen and this led to dilemmas around challenging homophobia while simultaneously tackling the stereotype that all tradeswomen, and indeed all feminists, were lesbians (Women and Manual Trades, 1978 and 1987). Alliances made with working-class men around issues such as labour exploitation and health and safety jarred on occasion with feminist politics (Women and Manual Trades, 1978).

The training schemes described in this chapter are only a selection of the many initiatives, and are chosen for the availability of information or their particular significance or high profile. One of the earliest schemes to be set up and therefore very important was the East Leeds Women's Workshop, founded in 1981 by Sandra McNeill. Miranda Miller from the Leeds Council for Voluntary Service provided office space and administration support for the workshop and the European Social Fund and Leeds City Council provided funding. McNeill insisted that childcare costs for students should be included in the ESF grant and this became adopted as a central element of all such funding. The workshop was run as a workers' co-operative. This fitted with its socialist and feminist ideology and admission to courses operated on a points system. Applicants were awarded two points for being black and one point for membership of other groups such as lesbians and single mothers, while disabled women were given absolute priority. In 1988 the workshop was awarded the Lady Platt Award for Equal Opportunities Training and by the time it closed in 1999 an average of 40 women a year had been trained, many of whom progressed into employment or self-employment or further training courses (personal correspondence).

In 1983 Claire Dove set up Blackburne House, originally called the Women's Technology and Education Centre, in the Merseyside Trade Union Centre. In 1989 the Centre became the first women's voluntary group to gain accreditation to offer a BTEC National Certificate in Computing and Blackburne House remains one of the leading women's education providers in Merseyside. The organisation provided over 1000 full and part-time learning opportunities in a variety of trades and technologies. It was awarded Beacon College status by the Department for Education and Skills, which involved disseminating its practices to other learning providers, and was repeatedly granted Grade 1 status by the Adult Learning Inspectorate (personal correspondence).

Women's Education in Building was established in 1984 to provide training for women choosing careers in the building trades. By 1994 it was the largest construction training centre in Europe and WEB courses were so over-subscribed that the organisation had a two-year waiting list. Trainees were offered tuition in maths and literacy as well as trades and could access a job placement scheme (Women's Education in Building, 1994, pp1, 5-6). The organisation had a 90 per cent completion rate for trainees, of whom 50 per cent were from ethnic minorities (Women's Education in Building, 1994, p7). Projects running in the early 2000s included Build Up, targeted at ethnic minority women, and Women Building London, funded by the European Social Fund to provide advice, information and support to 1,400 female trainees in the capital (European Social Fund, 2003). The organisation launched a women's business centre in 2003 but this went into liquidation the following year when it failed to gain funding from the Department of Trade and Industry (Women in London, 2004). Nottinghamshire Women's Training Scheme, funded by the local authority and the European Social Fund, was set up in 1985 to provide six month courses for women in manual trades (Business in the Community, 1989, p20). There was a particular focus on Black and Asian women, who made up at least 50 per cent of the trainees (Women and Manual Trades, 1985). The scheme closed in 1998 for reasons unknown but probably to do with difficulties in bidding for European Social Fund grants.

In 1988, Oxford City Council set up the Oxford Women's Training Scheme under the leadership of Jane Butcher. Courses in manual trades and IT were offered at the Northway Centre in Oxford and on various local housing estates. In 1996 the scheme became an Industrial and Provident Society run by its own staff and management committee, as the funding provided by the City Council gradually decreased. Projects and funding subsequently diversified and included a contract with the Learning and Skills Council for the provision of construction and IT training and involvement in the JIVE project. But funding problems continued and in 2005 the Scheme was incorporated into the newly expanded Oxford and Cherwell Valley College as a separate department for women. It also began to run a South East England Development Agency project for women in social enterprise, and partnered with Businesslink Solutions to deliver a South East Women's Mentoring Network for managers in small to medium-sized enterprises (Oxford City Council, 2006; personal correspondence).

In Wales, *Chwarae Teg* (Fair Play) was established in 1992 to promote the role of women in the national economy. The Ready, SET Go project was set up as part of the education and skills strand of the project, funded by the European Social Fund, *Chwarae Teg*, the Welsh Assembly and Careers Wales. Specialist women only training was developed in partnership with Further Education Institutions, in the form of taster courses run over a ten day period incorporating work placements. Three hundred women participated in the project between its inception in 2004 and its conclusion in 2007. An evaluation carried out at the end of the project was completed by 70 women, of whom 45 per cent had progressed into further training courses and 15 per cent directly into employment (personal correspondence).

As well as independent projects such as those described, several further education colleges provided women only training and campaigned around gender equality. In the mid-1980s Vauxhall College of Building and Further Education instituted an equal opportunities programme which included initiatives such as a two day residential course for lecturers in which appropriate teaching and learning strategies were discussed and developed, and women only courses in the trades (Vauxhall College of Building and Further Education, 1985). The Hull College project on women and construction also ran in the 1980s, working with local primary and secondary schools on the curriculum, providing a GNVQ foundation course on construction and the built environment at a local girls' school, raising awareness of women's potential as construction workers, providing short women only courses, developing a curriculum for women returners, using women lecturers as role models, and setting targets for female recruitment (General NVQ, 1996, p11). A project at Eastleigh College involved strategies such as using gender neutral language to describe construction related courses, using female staff as role models and mentors, organising summer schools for women and girls and promoting college taster days (General NVQ, 1996, p13).

However, by the end of the 1990s it was increasingly difficult to bid successfully for European Social Fund grants for women only training, as ESF had removed this as a specific funding category and now favoured large-scale projects. Member States' governments were made responsible for allocating funds, introducing additional agendas and layers of bureaucracy. Nevertheless, a number of initiatives continued or were started up with ESF funding and sponsorship from other sources. Colleges running women only courses for manual trades in the early and mid-2000s included North Devon College, Stockton Riverside College, Bexley College, Rotherham College of Arts and Technology, Sheffield College, Moulton College, Barnet College and Sparsholt College (UK Resource Centre for Women in SET, 2006b). Other organisations offering courses included Leicester City Council, Bristol Women's Workshop, the Plumbing Academy and Lambeth Women's workshop (Leicester City Council, 2006; UK Resource Centre for Women in SET, 2006b). Socially excluded women remained the target group with a number of courses targeted at specific groups such as Manchester's Wai Yin Chinese Women Society's Women Construction Solutions course which offered training in practical construction skills to Chinese women in a culturally sensitive environment (Wai Yin Chinese Women Society, 2006).

The South Yorkshire Women's Development Trust is an example of a large initiative which came into being at this time: it was launched in 2002 to provide support, resources and funding opportunities for women's organisations across South Yorkshire. This consortium of women's groups included Asian women's associations AWAZZ and LAIYIN and the Women's Cultural Club, all of which provided training courses including IT and basic maths and English. The Trust also offered three bespoke courses to approximately 300 women per year, including Women in Non-Traditional Trades and Technology (WINTT), set up in 2004 in partnership with Sheffield Hallam University and funded by the Learning and Skills Council and ESF. The Trust was offered premises in an old school free of charge on condition that students made improvements to the building. Around 100 new women per year registered for the course. An initial basic grounding in DIY was followed by a seven week intensive course in a specialised trade, taught by one of ten female instructors towards an accredited basic qualification. During the first three years of its operation many WINTT students progressed to further vocational training or employment in their chosen trade (personal correspondence).

Case Study 5.1: Women and Manual Trades (WAMT)

Women and Manual Trades was established in 1975 in London by a group of tradeswomen who wanted to provide their peers with support and representation (Women and Manual Trades, 2000, p1). By 1976 regional groups had been set up in Leeds and Bradford, Manchester and Edinburgh (Women and Manual Trades, 2000, p5). From the beginning WAMT was underpinned by an explicitly feminist politics although there was conflict over making alliances with feminism and socialism and how this might impact on the group's image and work (Women and Manual Trades, 1981). There was a WAMT stand and workshop at the National Women's Liberation conference in Newcastle in 1976 and in the late 1970s the group began working with feminist networks to repair women's refuges, which continued well into the 1990s (Women and Manual Trades, 1993 and 2000, pp2, 4). By 1983 WAMT was engaged in a programme of political campaigning and giving support to six separate sexual harassment cases (Women and Manual Trades, 2000, p11). It also involved itself with other issues such as imperialism, capitalism, and domestic and sexual violence. During the 1980s WAMT began to diversify its politics to include the issues of women with disabilities and black tradeswomen and at its 1987 conference the broadening focus of the wider women's movement was reflected in the issues of classism, racism, and anti-lesbianism (Women and Manual Trades, 2000, p15).

As well as its links to second wave radical feminism WAMT worked with liberal-feminist institutions such as the Equal Opportunities Commission, which in 1977 sponsored the production of literature for members and prospective members about training opportunities. In 1979 WAMT presented an exhibition at an Equal Opportunities Commission conference in Manchester on non-traditional careers for girls and, with EOC funding, produced a video and pamphlet for school leavers. In 1980 the Edinburgh branch embarked on an EOC-funded study of the situation for women training in the trades in Scotland (Women and Manual Trades, 2000, p3-7). In the 1980s WAMT was represented on a newly formed Labour Party working group on women's issues and involved with lobbying influential industry bodies such as the Construction Industry Training Board (CITB) (Women and Manual Trades, 2000, pp4, 8). Partly as a result of this lobbying, in the mid-1980s WAMT was asked to draw up an equal opportunities policy for the Manpower Services Commission, which reflected its influence in the political mainstream (Women and Manual Trades, 2000, p14).

By the 1980s there were WAMT groups in Nottingham, Bradford, Edinburgh and London. The organisation helped to set up a number of women's training workshops around the country, publicised services offered by tradeswomen and developed a programme of talks in schools as part of the GIST project (see Chapter Three). But by the late 1980s the climate was becoming increasingly difficult: many women's workshops were closing due to lack of funding, Direct Labour Organisations were in decline and in 1989 the Manpower Services Commission was dissolved, leaving WAMT to focus on equal opportunities in the new National Vocational Qualifications (NVQs) (Women and Manual Trades, 2000, p17, 19). The organisation was forced to adjust to the shift in construction opportunities to the private sector and accordingly developed a list of firms which were women-friendly (Women and Manual Trades, 2000, p19). During this new phase of operation WAMT began to develop its international links through IRIS, a new transnational network for women's training providers. As the climate for funding worsened and the women's movement fragmented, the national conference in 1991 focused on how to survive cutbacks. The organisation responded by merging with the Women in Construction Advisory Group (see Chapter Six), a survival strategy which seemed to work (Women and Manual Trades, 2000, p19).

During the 1990s WAMT was involved in several large funded projects, starting in 1993 with the Self-Employed Tradeswomen's Initiative which aimed to increase work opportunities for tradeswomen and in 1994 with Business Training for Tradeswomen. WAMT organised a European conference on women and employment in the construction industry and represented the UK in FORUM, the European Tradeswomen's Network, (Women and Manual Trades, 2000, p21, 23). Beginning in the late 1990s, the Tradeswomen into Site Supervision project trained women as site supervisors in partnership with groups in Copenhagen and Germany (Women and Manual Trades, 2000, p27). In 1999 a new transnational research project entitled Interventions focused on the recruitment of girls and young women to non-traditional fields (Women and Manual Trades 2000, pp28-29). WAMT developed an interest in environmentally friendly building and in 1998 launched a project entitled Introduction to Ecological Building for unemployed tradeswomen (Women and Manual Trades, 2000, pp26-27). The Building Work for Women project began in 1999 in the London area, giving female students practical experience in various trades (Pillbeam and Farren, 2004, p15).

In 2001, under the leadership of Karen Procter, the structure of WAMT shifted from feminist collective to director-led organisation and it embarked on a new period of collaboration with central government, first with the DTI Promoting SET for Women Unit and then with the UK Resource Centre for Women in SET (Women and Manual Trades, 2000, p30; Women and Manual Trades, 2001). In 2002 the organisation joined forces with the DTI and CITB on a new campaign to increase the number of women in construction by 2005 (Women and Manual Trades, 2002). WAMT projects continued into the mid-2000s: Upskill provided support for trainee and unemployed tradeswomen in London to enable them to access further training or become self-employed. Building Links into Employment ran from 2002 to 2004, helping 182 unemployed skilled tradeswomen into work in the London area, and DIY for Women offered free courses in painting and decorating, tiling, plumbing, carpentry and electrics in Spring 2006 (Women and Manual Trades, 2006).

Case study 5.2: The Women's Training Network
The Women's Training Network was formed in 1985 as an umbrella organisation for a variety of projects: women only training providers, networking and support organisations, guidance and counselling providers, projects working to change cultures in further and higher education and projects working with employers. The network was involved in setting up a large number of new women only training schemes and was instrumental in the proliferation of these schemes during the 1980s. There is little formal documentation and almost no analysis of WTN's work but it is estimated that between 1985 and 2000 at least 12,000 women benefited from its initiatives and over 40 groups and projects joined the network. Funding for the organisation was largely provided by local authorities who were sympathetic to positive action initiatives, with equivalent or matched funding from the European Social Fund (personal correspondence).

WTN politics drew from radical and lesbian feminist ideas about the benefits of women only environments, rejected the elitism of women's centres and academic feminism and sought to improve the material conditions of working-class women's lives through giving them skills and consciousness raising. WTN used tutors who were tradeswomen rather than trained teachers, since formally trained teachers were thought to have been trained by men in the context of racist and sexist structures. In line with the feminist slogan 'the personal is political', the training process was seen as more important than the outcome, meaning that the organisation focused on the quality of the training experience rather than whether beneficiaries were able to progress into employment. However, paid work was linked to liberation in the form of economic independence. Within the organisation itself, WTN sought to foster a democratic and non-hierarchical structure with collective decision making and even distribution of responsibilities (personal correspondence).

During the 1980s WTN supported women's training centres in many districts, towns and cities including Bath, Birmingham, Bradford, Bristol, Cambridge, Edinburgh, Leeds, Liverpool, Middlesborough, Milton Keynes, Nottingham, Sheffield, Tyneside and the London Boroughs of Camden, Haringey, Islington, Lambeth, Lewisham and Southwark. But cuts in funding, the central government shift towards boys and men as educational non-participants, the backlash against feminism and the fragmentation and academisation of the women's movement undermined the network's activities in the 1990s, causing staff redundancies and the resignation of three directors (personal correspondence). The economic and political climate for women's training did not improve and in the absence of core funding WTN administrative functions were delivered from 2001 onwards by the Oxford Women's Training Scheme. At this time WTN became more focused on national and European policy. As a core partner in the JIVE project WTN shifted towards influencing national and pan-European training policy agendas through European Social Fund committees and liaison with the Equal Opportunities Commission, the Learning and Skills Council, government departments and Regional Development Agencies (personal correspondence).

Case study 5.3: Let's TWIST and JIVE Partners
In 1998 Annette Williams founded the Let's TWIST project at Bradford College, in partnership with Ros Wall at Sheffield Hallam University. It focused broadly on promoting women's participation in SECT and more specifically on the manual trades and women's training. The project's services for women included support and mentoring and the provision of careers information and guidance, as well as staff development training in gender equality and consultancy and advice to employers, colleges, universities and careers companies. The main feature of the project was women only training courses in a range of trades, taught at Bradford College. The courses were between 12 weeks and a year long and were geared at various basic qualifications and taught by specially trained female tutors. As with other such schemes the target group was socially excluded women, and childcare and travel costs were provided. In a context in which such monies were difficult to obtain, Let's TWIST was in receipt of funding from the European Social Fund, the European Leonardo da Vinci fund, the Construction Industry

Training Board and the Yorkshire and Humber Regional Development Agency (Let's TWIST, 2001; personal communication).

The politics and practices of Let's TWIST made use of the radical feminist framework which focused on the masculine culture of manual trades and aimed to empower women through teaching them traditionally masculine skills (Aschauer, 1999). The pedagogic approach incorporated working with women's particular yet diverse learning styles, encouraging collaboration rather than competition, acknowledging women's achievements and making learning relevant to their experiences, developing a mixture of practical and active intellectual learning techniques. The importance of offering women practical and emotional support was recognised. The project was organised around the feminist idea of 'women helping women' (Haywoode, 1983, p56) and incorporated not only the women only educational environment but also a team of managerial and administrative staff who were predominantly female (personal communication). An independent evaluation of Let's TWIST, conducted in 2003, found that this model inspired a positive response in terms of the development of skills and confidence and also the opportunity to become conscious of and resist disempowering constructions of femininity (Phipps, 2005).

Let's TWIST diverged from the standard formulation of women's training by growing in scale and engaging more centrally with the corporate world. This was largely undertaken under the aegis of the Joint Intervention (JIVE) Partnership which was funded by the European Social Fund under the EQUAL initiative. Through this partnership and at a time in which other women's training schemes were faced with disastrous funding cuts, the Let's TWIST team were able to shape their work to fit new policy and corporate agendas. Partners in JIVE included the Women's Training Network, the Engineering Construction Industry Training Board, the Equal Opportunities Commission, the Oxford Women's Training Scheme, Women's Education in Building and the Open University, as well as European partners in Denmark, Finland, France, and Germany (Pillbeam and Farren, 2004, p17; Andrew, 2005, pii). JIVE activities focused on disseminating good practice and reforming industry cultures and were delivered through regional hubs including Yorkshire and Humber, the south east, and Wales (Andrew, 2005). Staff supported female students and SECT professionals, offered guidance to employers and policy-makers and trained educators to develop a conducive learning environment (Pillbeam and Farren, 2004, p17; JIVE, 2006). In 2004 the success of Annette Williams and her team was recognised when they were selected by the Office of Science and Technology to create a UK Resource Centre for Women in SET (see Chapter Six).

2. Women's literacy in ICT

The issue of women's training in technology, particularly in information and communication technologies (ICT), came to prominence in the 1990s and 2000s with certain groups of women being identified as in need of particular support. This was linked to the government agenda around the information society or the penetration of ICTs into every aspect of working and domestic life. As well the aim of making the UK the world's leading Internet economy, an important concern grew around social inclusion for people who could not fully exploit the potential of ICT and could therefore become further socially excluded. This agenda was linked to but separate from issues around women's participation in ICT professions (see Chapter Four), focusing mainly on the use and not the design of ICTs. The concept of the digital divide was used to symbolise differing patterns of ICT use dependent on factors such as gender, class, age and ethnicity.

Women's computer access was slightly lower than that of men in 1999: 51 per cent of women had used a PC compared with 66 per cent of men. Women were more likely to lack confidence with computing equipment and to question its relevance to their everyday lives (Department of Trade and Industry, 1999, p1). Table 5.2 on page 110 shows levels of awareness and use of PCs and the Internet in the late 1990s broken down by gender.

Women's access to and use of ICTs were better than their position in technician level employment due to the proliferation of technologies for home use, more and more products targeted at women and more girls and young women becoming computer literate (Faulkner, 2004, p29). Table 5.3 on page 110 shows women's employment in technical and sales jobs in the ICT and electronics sector in 1999. Their representation among manufacturing workers did not rise above 38 per cent in broadcasting and telecoms equipment manufacture and was at its lowest in the manufacture of industrial equipment. In sales women's representation stood at 28 per cent in all categories, perhaps because wholesalers generally sold a varied range of equipment.

In 1999 the UK government commissioned several reports on social exclusion and ICTs under the aegis of the Policy Action Team. The PAT 15 process, as it was called, was intended to gather information and make

Table 5.2 Awareness and use of PCs and the Internet 1996 and 1998

		% of Women		% of Men	
		1996	1998	1996	1998
Aware of	PC	90	96	93	95
	Internet	90	96	94	97
Have used	PC	42	51	61	66
	Internet	8	22	19	35

(Department of Trade and Industry, 1999, p3)

Table 5.3 Employment in skilled technical ICT jobs 1999

	% Women	% Men
Manufacturing		
Manufacture of office machinery	29	71
Manufacture of computers and computer equipment	32	68
Manufacture of insulated wire and cable	23	77
Manufacture of electronic components	37	63
Manufacture of TV and radio transmitters and telecoms equipment	27	73
Manufacture of TV and radio receivers and equipment	38	62
Manufacture of industrial equipment	24	76
Sales		
Wholesale of ICT Products	28	72
Wholesale of electrical appliances & radio & TV goods	28	72
Wholesale of office machinery and equipment	28	72
Wholesale of other machinery for use in industry	28	72

(Department of Trade and Industry, 1999, p12)

recommendations on best practice in providing access to ICTs and ICT skills for citizens in disadvantaged areas. There was a particular focus on Internet use due to the rapid growth in email and World Wide Web applications and the migration of services such as banking, travel, job-seeking and some areas of education to online spaces. Women Connect, a network of women's voluntary and community organisations led by Marion Scott and Margaret Page, was commissioned to represent women in the PAT 15 process. They organised a seminar for women's organisations, the Women's Unit and the Women's National Commission, and other interested parties. The report produced from this seminar provided an overview of women's ICT needs and recommendations for appropriate provision. These included mainstreaming issues of women and ICTs throughout government policy, building capacity in terms of training and ICT resources for local women's centres and services, investing in good quality and accessible childcare and creating sustainable funding patterns for initiatives (Women Connect, 1999).

a. Gender and community informatics

In 1996 the UK government launched a national information society initiative which positioned ICTs within a discourse around economic, political and social development. Adult education was thought to be the key to improving access, with a particular focus on groups such as lone parents, people with disabilities, low qualified or unqualified people and members of some ethnic minority groups (Devins *et al*, 2002, p942; Selwyn and Gorard, 2003, p171). A number of government-backed initiatives were set up such as UK online centres, Wired up Communities, and learndirect, and were delivered through home access to ICTs, schools and colleges, and learning centres in disadvantaged communities (Devins *et al*, 2002, p942; Selwyn and Gorard, 2003, p178). Gender was scarcely considered (Faulkner, 2004), perhaps because factors such as class and ethnicity were more important determinants of ICT access and use and reflecting the backlash against feminism and the shift in education policy towards the needs of boys and men. But women's groups were able to attach themselves to the information society agenda with initiatives targeted at low-income, ethnic minority and lone parent women. The reliance of government on the voluntary and community sector to develop local ICT access projects meant that women's groups were able to gain support under this community informatics agenda and sponsorship from official bodies (Loader and Keeble, 2004, p1).

Long before the launch of this information society initiative and the awakening of official interest in the issue of women's use of ICT, some cutting-edge women's ICT training projects were put in place in the public and voluntary sectors. These differed from courses for women in manual trades in focusing on women's general ICT literacy as well as and in some cases instead of their progression into ICT employment. Nevertheless, the trades and ICT agendas were often combined as part of the feminist politics and ideas about social inclusion which under-pinned the work of many women's training centres, and training in manual trades and ICTs often took place under the same roof. Many of the perceived barriers were similar such as the lack of financial re-sources and appropriate childcare, women's lack of skills, knowledge and confidence and their belief that ICT had no value or relevance to their lives (Faulkner, 2004, pp7-8). Specialist women's ICT projects were characterised by the feminist pedagogic approaches and the elements such as fee waivers and help with childcare costs which were part of the projects for women in manual trades. The target groups were the same: unemployed and socially excluded women who found it difficult to access mainstream training. These women were trained in basic com-puting and office skills and often learned skills in computer networking and worked towards qualifications such as the European Computer Driving Licence. The courses were taught by supportive female tutors and incorporated elements of personal development, confidence building, consciousness raising and work experience.

In 1982 the Cambridge Women's Resource Centre was set up by a group of women academics trying to mitigate the masculine culture of the university and improve women's under-representation in the IT industry. Cambridge City Council provided grant funding and support also came from the Manpower Services Commission, the European Social Fund and the Equal Opportunities Commission. The first courses to be offered were computer programming and computer technology, a curriculum which broadened to include health, home maintenance, carpentry and basic maths and IT, as the primary goal of improving women's labour market participation shifted in response to more fundamental needs among the client group. The centre was one of the first in the country to provide free on-site childcare. By the mid-2000s around 500 women per year were registering for training although the loss of ESF sponsorship in 2005 threatened the centre with closure (personal correspondence).

In 1984 EOC Chairman Baroness Platt of Writtle and a group of Labour MPs including Rhodri Morgan, Jane Hutt and Alun Michael created the South Glamorgan Women's Workshop. The European Social Fund, South Glamorgan County Council and the Vale of Glamorgan Borough Council provided funding. In addition to its general technology training courses, the workshop developed specialist provision for women from ethnic minority groups. Its on-site crèche was then the only free crèche in Wales. To supplement its funds the workshop offered self-financed training to women who were not eligible for free courses and in-house training to employers. During its first ten years the workshop was positively evaluated by the Equal Opportunities Commission and the Department of Employment, featured in several publications as an example of good practice in women's training and won a number of awards. By the mid-2000s the workshop was training around 200 women per year and had become a partner in the trans-national JIVE project (Coats, 1996, pp38-40; personal correspondence).

Caroline Gregory and Annie Rafferty set up the Women's Technology and Enterprise Centre in Tameside in 1987 with funding from the local authority and the European Social Fund. During its ten years of operation the Centre trained forty women per year, most of whom progressed into further or higher education or straight into employment. The feminist politics of the Centre often led these trainees to question or change their personal lives. By the late 1990s funding became increasingly difficult and the Centre's site was sold. Once relocated it became a more generic learndirect location (personal communication). Also in the 1990s, the Fife Women's Technology Centre was set up as Dunfermline Women's Training Centre with funding provided by Dunfermline District Council and the European Social Fund. Over 450 women were trained at the centre between 1990 and the mid-2000s. Success was measured in terms of progression into work or further training as well as the trainees' personal development: according to these criteria the centre had an 80 per cent success rate. But by the early 2000s its existence was threatened by difficulty in obtaining funding and the backlash against women only projects (personal correspondence).

In 1992 Clem Herman led a group of women in setting up the Manchester Women's Electronic Village Hall with sponsorship from Manchester City Council, the Centre for Employment Research and Manchester Polytechnic. This was a dedicated training suite initially housed in a local community centre. There were originally two full-time and two part-time trainee tutors, delivering varied courses in ICT. Over the first two years the staff grew to fifteen and began to deliver outreach classes in other neighbourhoods. In 2002 the Women's Electronic Village Hall relocated to a new building in Manchester City centre and continued to provide ICT training for women into the mid-2000s. The initiative was deemed successful in terms of women trainees' acquisition of skills and confidence, the networks the women built up, and their moving into employment (personal correspondence)

Colleges offered women only foundation and vocational courses in ICT during the 1990s and early 2000s, including: Stourbridge, Doncaster, Hillcroft, Stockton Riverside, Llandrillo, Newham, Ealing Hammersmith and West London, City and Islington, Salford, the College of North West London, Faringdon Area Community College, City College Manchester, Dudley College of Technology and the North West Institute of Further and Higher Education in Northern Ireland. So did the universities of Limerick, Abertay, Dundee and Wolverhampton, and other organisations put on courses, including the Mary Ward Centre in London, the East London Advanced Technology Training organisation, Women's Computer Centre Limited, Alloa Women's Technology Centre, MiTech at Midlothian Council and the YWCA (UK Resource Centre for Women in SET, 2006b). Some of these courses were aimed at specific groups such as the IT for Bengali Women course at Portsmouth College, a course at London's Selby Centre for Asian women and courses for asylum seekers, refugee women, and Asian women at the YWCA. Silver Surfers at Peterborough Women's Centre was targeted at women over 50 and the computer workshop at the Manchester Education Resettlement Centre targeted women who had mental illnesses, problems with drugs or alcohol, or who had been involved with the criminal justice system (YWCA, 2005; UK Resource Centre for Women in SET, 2006b).

Case Study 5.5: Edinburgh Women's Training Centre

In 1986 the Edinburgh District Council set up the Edinburgh Women's Training Centre with funding provided by the European Social Fund, the City of Edinburgh Council and Telford College. The project was driven by the council strategies for the economy and social inclusion, aiming to increase the pool of skilled workers for the city's growing microelectronics economy and to meet demands for a variety of workers with IT skills (Faulkner and Kleif, 2003, p11). The Edinburgh Women's Training Course was launched in 1986 as the flagship project of the Centre and was the first women only ICT training project in Scotland (Faulkner and Kleif, 2003). The decision to launch the course was driven by pragmatic rather than political concerns since ESF was providing funding for such projects. It was set up by council representative John Fairley and prominent local feminists. All the course management and teaching staff were women, and this invited accusations of discrimination against men (Faulkner and Kleif, 2003, p12).

From its inception the Edinburgh Women's Training course recruited twenty-four women per year, most of them unemployed and with no relevant qualifications. They were positioned on one or more axes of disadvantage: lone parents, returners, women over 40, disabled women, women from ethnic minorities and women from areas of high unemployment (NISUS Scotland, 2003). Participants were required to be motivated to achieve, and this was generally assessed on taster courses prior to their enrolment (Faulkner and Kleif, 2003, pp3, 17). Free training was provided for five days per week over a full school year and participants were entitled to free travel and childcare (Faulkner and Kleif, 2003, p3). The original objective of the course was to train the women to take up employment in the traditionally male fields of computing technology and electronics but from 1992 the focus of the training shifted to user level ICT, with graduates generally progressing into traditionally female jobs in administration. This was because the emphasis on specialist ICT discouraged some women. It also reflected pressures around continued funding, in particular the need to provide a qualification such as the European Computer Driving License (Faulkner and Kleif, 2003, pp3, 12-13; NISUS Scotland, 2003).

The course adopted an interactive and student-led approach. Teaching was delivered in small women only groups and led by supportive female tutors. Students were encouraged to work at their own pace and developing self-esteem and confidence was considered as important as skills. The training incorporated a work placement with one of fifteen local employers in the public, private or voluntary sectors (Faulkner and Kleif, 2003, pp3, 19-23; NISUS Scotland, 2003). The aim was to create a sense of solidarity among the women on the course which, it was hoped, would foster student retention (Faulkner and Kleif, 2003, p20). The implicit contract was that training, childcare and travel would be provided free in return for students' commitment to attend and complete the course (Faulkner and Kleif, 2003, p14). Technology was labelled in instrumental terms as a set of tools and a route into employment. The course documentation avoided gendering particular technologies and gave no hint that technology was something women should be afraid of (Faulkner and Kleif, 2003, p16).

The length of the course enabled students to achieve reasonable levels of competence in ICT (Faulkner and Kleif, 2003, p3). During the early years in which the focus was specialist ICT employment, students progressed into the sector. Up to 90 per cent applied for jobs at technician level and a few achieved professional careers (Faulkner and Kleif, 2003, p25). From the early 1990s many course graduates, now proficient users of ICTs, went into further training or employment, albeit in traditionally feminine administrative careers (Faulkner and Kleif, 2003, p27). In the early 2000s 90 per cent of trainees gained vocational qualifications, 70 per cent completed work placements, 55 per cent securing employment, and 25 per cent moved into further education (Faulkner and Kleif, 2003, pp3, 23-24). Anecdotal evidence testified to the students' increased confidence (Faulkner and Kleif, 2003; p24, 27). In a user evaluation carried out in 2002, trainees described the transformative effect of the course in terms of either their employment circumstances or, more frequently, the way they saw themselves (Kleif and Faulkner, 2003).

The Edinburgh Women's Training Centre and its women only ICT course was a successful initiative which was launched for pragmatic reasons but which incorporated a variety of feminist ideas. The positive experiences of trainees can be attributed to several factors including the teaching approach, the safety and solidarity of the women only environment, the focus on confidence as well as skills, the choice of participants with aptitude and motivation, the financial help provided to them, and the implicit contract requiring their commitment. In the changing funding climate of the early 1990s the Centre shifted to mixed-sex training and commercial courses to generate income (Faulkner and Kleif, 2003, p13). The women's training course was reduced from five days per week to three (Faulkner and Kleif, 2003, p13) and the collectivist organisation of the Centre shifted towards a hierarchical structure and a new agenda of reporting, monitoring and accountability (Faulkner and Kleif, 2003, p13). Although the women's training course continued to run into the 2000s, its future appeared uncertain.

3. Discussion

The women only training projects described in this chapter blended liberal feminist ideas around equal opportunities with elements which came under the radical feminist banner of 'the personal is political', such as consciousness raising and assertiveness training (Coats, 1994, pp20-23; Zukas, 1998, p30). Projects often incorporated a critique of the masculinity of SECT cultures and attempts to reform them or to create alternative cultures inside women only space. Women were conceived as a group, defined in opposition to men and with common threads linking them together (Zukas, 1998, p28). Training women in non-traditional skills was seen as a way of empowering them to change their lives and resist the ways in which patriarchal society encouraged them to remain helpless. The pedagogic approaches drew on feminist ideas such as: starting from students' experiences and recognising the emotional as well as intellectual aspects of learning; enhancing women's confidence in their existing skills; developing an awareness of women's differences along the lines of class, sexuality, ethnicity and disability; using participatory teaching approaches; and constantly developing pedagogic practices with the aid of student feedback (Coats, 1994).

As well as incorporating liberal and radical feminist ideas, women only training drew from both liberal and radical traditions of adult education. The liberal tradition was focused on individual personal development, validating the experience and knowledge of the student and informal and student-centred delivery, while the radical tradition focused on social change, targeted disadvantaged groups, and identified with social movements (Benn, Elliott and Whaley, 1998, p2). The projects were mainly aimed at socially excluded women who had difficulty accessing mainstream training and education and who preferred routes back into learning which were informal, women-centred, and locally based (McGivney, 1998, p13). Account was taken of the personal and practical constraints on these women's educational participation and attempts were made to tackle structural barriers by providing fee waivers, free travel and childcare (Coats, 1994; McGivney, 1998, p14; Zukas, 1998, p29).

Among the problems the projects faced were being seen as inferior soft options by the mainstream educational establishment and being criticised for ghettoising and further marginalising women in the wider political context (Benn, 1998, p44; Women into Computing, 1988, p81). The effectiveness of women only training often rested heavily on the experience, attitude and commitment of individual trainers (Faulkner, 2004, p18). In addition, the radical feminist underpinnings of many of the projects sometimes discouraged support and funding. Yet despite their radical image, the dominant approach of most projects centred on empowering individual women rather than challenging the gender order. The key goal was personal rather than political change, a thera-peutic attempt to help women to change their own lives through build-ing skills and confidence (Coats, 1994, pp26-27). Within these para-meters positive results were reported of the personal development of the women and their progression into further training and employ-ment.

During the 1990s and 2000s women only training became mired in shifting financial structures and a hostile political climate. Changing funding regimes during the 1990s and 2000s negatively affected grass-roots initiatives, as did the growing emphasis within adult education on outcome-related learning and accreditation (Faulkner, 2004, p19; McGivney, 1998, pp9-10, 15). The Conservative government was re-emphasising the importance of home and family for women, alongside a backlash against feminism and equal opportunities initiatives in general (Benn, 1998, p45). It is poignant that partly because of the success of feminist initiatives in mainstream education and lifelong learning, boys and men became conceptualised as the new educational non-participants (Francis, 1999; Skelton, 1998). Women-only training virtually disappeared in the 2000s, and although some projects such as Let's TWIST and Women and Manual Trades adapted to the new context, questions could be raised about this pragmatism and abandonment of radicalism (Faulkner and Kleif, 2003).

The past three decades saw a decline in women's representation among workers in the construction industry. Table 5.4 shows the figures for women's participation in the late 1990s, which peaked in 1996 at 21 per cent of employees including administrative and associate workers, while among the self-employed, who tended to be tradespeople, it never rose above 3 per cent.

Table 5.4 Women's representation in the construction industry 1995-1999

	Employees		Self-employed	
	% Women	% Men	% Women	% Men
1995	18	82	2	98
1996	21	79	3	97
1997	14	86	2	98
1998	15	85	3	97
1999	14	86	2	98

(Department of Trade and Industry, 2006a, p151)

By the early 2000s, women were gaining more vocational qualifications than men but formed a tiny minority of students in engineering, technology, construction and property and a large majority of students in hairdressing and beauty therapy (Gurjao, 2006, pp10-11). A few tradeswomen worked in local authority building departments or direct labour organisations but, as shown in Table 5.5, little had changed since the 1970s in the skilled manual trades, with women's representation often standing at less than 1 per cent (Clarke et al, 2005, p161).

In 2002, women constituted only 3 per cent of trainees entering craft and technical construction courses (Gurjao, 2006, p16). Ten per cent of the total construction workforce was female but they represented over 80 per cent of secretaries and administrators (Gurjao, 2006, p2). By 2003

Table 5.5 Women's representation in various skilled trades 2001

	Women as			
	% of employees	% of trainees	% of self-employed	% of total
Wood Trades	0.3	0.1	0	0.2
Bricklayers	0.1	0	0	0.1
Plasterers	0	0	0.1	0.1
Roofers	0	0	0.8	0.3
Painters & decorators	0.6	0.4	1.1	0.8
Scaffolders	0.05	0.5	0.4	0.1
Electricians	0	2.4	0	0
Plumbers	0	0	0	0
Maintenance	0.4	0	0	0.3
General Operatives	0.01	0	0	0.1
Total	0.2	0.2	0.2	0.2

(Clarke and Wall, 2004, p43)

the number of women in the construction workforce had dropped to 9 per cent and they made up only 1 per cent of tradespeople, 2 per cent of sole traders, 4 per cent of those running microenterprises, 10 per cent of those working in professional occupations such as design and management, and a massive 84 per cent of secretarial staff (Gurjao, 2006, p16).

Women's participation in technician-level ICT employment in the early 2000s was better in numerical terms than in manual trades, although percentages had remained stable since the late 1990s. In 2001 women made up 30 per cent of IT operations technicians and 32 per cent of IT user support technicians (Ellen and Herman, 2005, p8). But their use of ICT improved vastly by 2006. Men's and women's Internet usage levels were 65 and 55 per cent respectively, although 40 per cent of women had never used the Internet compared to 30 per cent of men (National Statistics, 2006, p3, 5). These figures were a significant increase on the Internet usage statistics of 1999 and reflect the success of women-only

ICT training schemes. However, the contrast between women's use of ICT and their representation in the manual trades may be more appropriately attributed to the unshakeable masculinity of the construction sector and the incursion of ICT into almost every aspect of public and private life.

Cynthia Cockburn (1983, 1985) and other feminists argue that that gender, trades and technologies and capitalism have been inextricably interlinked throughout history and that notions of skill became gendered through complex strategies of inclusion and exclusion which were rooted in both gender and class power. Trades and technical skills became male property through a social shaping process in which they were associated with particular traits such as rationality, physical strength and mastery over nature, which were also central to the conceptualisation of masculinity. The relations between gender and craft and technological fields are thus manifested both structurally and culturally in terms of men's control of these domains and symbolically in terms of gendered categories and identities (Faulkner, 2001, p81).

As well as addressing structural and individual barriers and engaging with SECT cultures, training projects for women could arguably have deconstructed the symbolic equivalence between masculinity and technical and craft skills as part of the curriculum. Instead of women appropriating masculine skills, the association of masculinity with qualities such as technical skill, physical strength and confidence, and the construction of women as lacking these characteristics could have been systematically challenged. In an independent evaluation of Let's TWIST in 2003, a sample of nine trainees reported that learning craft skills had enabled them to develop confidence and contemplate new careers. Yet they did not display a sense of ownership of the skills they had acquired and conceptualised themselves as having achieved a great deal as women but as less skilled than men (Phipps, 2005).

This sample cannot be fully representative of the broad mass of projects. The trainees' responses should properly be attributed to external factors as well as those internal to the Let's TWIST initiative. Nevertheless, this small-scale study raises questions about how far teaching masculine skills can empower women if the masculinity of these skills is not subject to critical analysis. In contrast, the community informatics framework on which many of the women only ICT projects were based was characterised by women shaping and reshaping ICTs for their own use (Loader and Keeble, 2004, p4). This was consistent with feminist thinking around the social shaping of technology, and could be seen as a step towards developing a curriculum which would address this issue. However, there is a need to go a step further, and to encourage women to take ownership of craft and technical skills through disentangling how they are reliant on masculinity and vice versa.

6

The business case for equality
State and corporate agendas for women in SECT

Education and training in the UK has always been closely linked to the needs of the economy and the assumption has generally been that it should be at the service of business rather than the other way around (Arnot, 2002; Gleeson and Keep, 2004). From the 1960s, SECT education and training in particular was linked with government concerns about the supply of skilled labour. The 1959 Crowther Report positioned education as an investment in national efficiency and argued for a broadening of the curriculum in scientific and technological areas (Central Advisory Council for Education, 1959). The 1963 Newsom Report recommended that the science curriculum should be made more relevant to the needs of pupils of differing abilities and drew attention to their unrealised talent (Central Advisory Committee for Education, 1963).

During the early 1990s, a more explicit concern with women's participation in SECT emerged in both government and corporate circles in the context of economic globalisation processes and issues for Western industrialised states around maintaining a competitive position in the global market place. Government and corporate initiatives were driven by a case for promoting women's participation in SECT which focused on the benefits women could bring to SECT industries. This chapter explores these initiatives, questioning the alliance between economic and social justice concerns and commenting on the appropriateness of the state and industry as agents of gender equality.

1. State feminism, mainstreaming and diversity

The growth of state involvement in promoting women's participation in SECT occurred during a period of heightened awareness of women's issues and when increasing official commitments were made to women's equality at national and international levels. In 1946 the United Nations Commission on the Status of Women (CSW) had been established as part of the Economic and Social Council with a brief to prepare recommendations and reports on promoting women's rights in political, economic, civil, social and educational fields (Division for the Advancement of Women, 2006a). Almost thirty years later the first United Nations World Conference on Women was held during International Women's Year in 1975 in Mexico City. The UN Convention on the Elimination of All Forms of Discrimination against Women (CEDAW) was adopted in 1979: in ratifying the convention states became legally bound to put its provisions into practice and to submit national reports on the measures they had taken towards women's equality. The United Kingdom ratified the Convention in 1986 (Division for the Advancement of Women, 2006b).

In the UK context and just prior to the first national Women's Liberation conference in 1971, the Women's National Commission was established in 1969. This umbrella organisation was created to represent women and women's organisations throughout the UK and to act as an independent, albeit fully government-funded, advisory body to the government on women's issues (Women's National Commission, 2005). After this institutional commitment two significant pieces of gender equality legislation were enacted: the Equal Pay Act of 1970 and the Sex Discrimination Act of 1975. Direct and indirect sex discrimination became unlawful and the Equal Opportunities Commission was created to monitor the progress of the law. After a long period of Thatcherism, the Labour government set up the Women's Unit in the 1900s, which in 1997 became the Women and Equality Unit, within the Department of Trade and Industry. This unit supported the Ministers for Women, who were responsible for developing gender equality policy, but it was poorly resourced and had little influence on policy (Squires and Wickham-Jones, 2004).

There were a number of government initiatives around equal pay and employment rights in the early 2000s: Fair Pay Champions were appointed from business, the public sector and trades unions to share examples of good practice and the Castle Awards were presented in 2002 to recognise employers' efforts regarding equal pay and opportunities (Women and Equality Unit, 2006). The Work-Life balance campaign begun in 2000 was directed at employers. It aimed to convince them of the case for change and to promote good practice (Women and Equality Unit, 2006). The Employment Act of 2002 extended maternity rights, granted new rights to fathers and put in place a framework for flexible working. In the same year the government set a Public Service Agreement (PSA) target on gender equality for 2008 which sought to reduce the pay gap and improve women's labour market participation (Office of Science and Technology, 2003). In 2004 the Women and Work commission was set up to report to the government on the gender pay gap (Women and Equality Unit, 2006).

In the 1990s there was much discussion in the United Nations and European Commission of the idea of gender mainstreaming: how could gender issues be embedded into mainstream policy and practice (Walby, 2002; Daly, 2005, pp433-5)? Mainstreaming was officially launched as a policy principle at the UN World Conference on Women in Beijing in 1995 and in 1997 the member states of the European Union signed up to a system of policy-making which required a gender mainstreaming approach (Rubery, 2005, p1). The UK government officially adopted mainstreaming as its gender policy in 1998 (Squires and Wickham-Jones, 2004, p81). Mainstreaming advocates saw this as a radical and transformative approach requiring wholesale redesigning of systems and structures in the service of gender equality (see for example Rees, 2001, 2005). In practice however, the primary incentive for adopting mainstreaming was often policy modernisation rather than gender equality and many mainstreaming approaches generated little change (Daly, 2005, pp440, 448; Perrons, 2005, p390). In the UK mainstreaming was confined to a few policy domains and marginal bodies such as the Women and Equality Unit, although in 2007 the government instituted a gender duty for public bodies such as health and police authorities, schools and universities and government departments which required them to demonstrate that they were treating men and women fairly rather than it resting with individuals to make complaints about discrimination (Daly, 2005, p435, 439; Equal Opportunities Commission, 2007).

Within industry broad economic developments created an increasing demand for women's labour. The shift from manufacturing to services and knowledge-based production, together with the emergence of new sectors of information and communication technologies, global finance and biotechnologies meant that by 2000 the landscape within which companies operated had shifted (Acker, 2004, p19). An increasingly flexible and multi-skilled labour force was required to cope with this new economy, and diversity of employees became seen as an economic resource. In a trend which began in North America and spread across Europe, companies sought out diverse skills, perspectives and ways of working in order to stimulate creative exchange and to ensure that they could recruit from the widest possible talent pool (Point and Singh, 2003, p751; Wrench, 2005, p78). There was also a belief that diversity within corporations would reflect and attract a diversity of customers (Point and Singh, 2003, p751). Under-represented groups such as women, ethnic minorities and people with disabilities were targeted and it was believed that this 'melting pot or cultural mosaic' would bring significant business benefits (Blackmore 2006, p184).

2. High Tide: women in SECT and the state from the 1990s

The British government became involved in the issue of women's participation in SECT against this broad political and economic canvas. The Finniston Report, launched in 1980, focused on how the UK could produce a better calibre of graduates in scientific and technical fields and identified a need to attract more girls to widen the talent pool (Ellis, 2003, p11). Following this the Equal Opportunities Commission and the Engineering Council designated 1984 as Women into Science and Engineering (WISE) year. The 1984 WISE Education and Training Conference represented the coalition of groups and individuals in government, education and industry which had begun to form. The speakers included the Director-General of the National Economic Development Office, the President of the Women's Engineering Society, the Technical Director of General Electric plc and the Chair of the Equal Opportunities Commission (Women into Science and Engineering, 1984). In the same year the Women's National Commission published its report *The Other Half of Our Future*, and hosted a conference for representatives of women's organisations, industry and education at which the keynote speakers included the Secretary of State for Employment and the Chairman of the Engineering Industry Training Board (Cabinet Office, 1984, piv).

The idea that women's participation in SECT would bring economic benefits became increasingly popular and gender equality was re-positioned in terms of national economic competitiveness. This process was expedited in the 1990s when the agenda of the Department for Education and Skills was dictated by the issue of boys' underachievement and concerns about women in SECT were taken up by other government departments, in particular the Department of Trade and Industry (Skelton, 1998; Francis, 1999). Instead of a focus on girls' and young women's experiences of science and technology education (see Chapter Three) there was a shift towards improving the supply of SECT professionals in industry and academia. This was underpinned by the conceptualisation of women as a valuable and under-used source of labour, which was used strategically by some feminists and women's groups to draw attention to their cause (personal communication).

A business-led and government-backed initiative, Opportunity 2000 was set up in 1991. It aimed to increase women's employment opportunities. Organisations paid a fee to join the campaign, in return for which they were given support with setting goals for women's equality and monitoring their progress towards these goals. In collaboration with the Department of Trade and Industry the Opportunity 2000 campaign produced a booklet addressing the issue of Women in SECT entitled *Making the Most: Women in Science, Engineering, and Technology*. This was aimed at the business community and contained case studies of good employment practice (Department of Trade and Industry and Opportunity, 2000, 1995). The campaign's website, *Tapping the Talent*, presented further examples of good business practice for women in SECT (Opportunity, 2000, 1996). In the 2000s, the initiative changed its name to Opportunity Now (Business in the Community, 2006).

A report to the Department of Employment in 1991 forecast that the construction industry would need to recruit from a wider labour pool to cope with even a moderate growth in output (Women's Education in Building, 1994, p2). In 1995 the Chartered Institute of Building and the Department of the Environment commissioned an action plan for gender equality in the building professions (Institute of Employment Studies, 1995).

a. Promoting SET for Women

The White Paper of 1993 *Realising Our Potential* constituted the first major statement of UK science policy for over twenty years (Office of Science and Technology, 1993). The document was structured by ideas about the importance of science and technology to Britain's future economic growth and the centrality of human capital to the development of the science and technology base. It argued for a better fit between industry and science and technology education and although it did not address gender issues in SECT, women were positioned as the country's most under-valued human resource within its economic rationale (Office of Science and Technology, 1993). In response, an independent group of mainly women SECT professionals was set up in 1994, chaired by Chief Scientific Adviser William Stewart, to produce the report *The Rising Tide* (Committee on Women in Science, Engineering, and Technology, 1994). Cambridge academic Nancy Lane, senior civil servant Jan Peters and AWiSE founder Joan Mason were part of the group. Their report tapped in to the economic rationale for women's equality, arguing that increasing women's representation in science, engineering and technology was crucial to maintain competitiveness and quality of life (Committee on Women in Science, Engineering, and Technology, 1994; personal communication).

The major recommendation of *The Rising Tide* was for the government to create a unit dedicated to the promotion of women's participation in science, engineering and technology, located within the Office of Science and Technology (Committee on Women in Science, Engineering, and Technology, 1994). Accordingly, the Promoting SET for Women Unit was set up in 1994. The idea was for the unit to function as a facilitatory body, providing an impetus for projects and co-ordinating existing groups and initiatives at grassroots level. It was envisaged that it would work with NGOs, quangos, government departments and research councils to identify and disseminate good practice and to raise public awareness of women's contribution to science, engineering and technology (Office of Science and Technology, 1994). The Unit had a small budget with which to support grassroots activities and was in a position to mediate between the activist community and other funding agencies (personal communication).

The Promoting SET for Women Unit developed and delivered several initiatives. Much of its work involved collating and disseminating the results of existing activity: in 1997 it published a report entitled *Breaking the Mould* which summarised a range of strategies which were already in place (Vlaeminke *et al*, 1997). It co-sponsored the production of Josephine Warrior's handbook *Cracking It!*, which contained tips for women who aspired to a SECT career (Warrior, 1997). The Unit provided funding for existing and new initiatives such as the Royal Society's Rosalind Franklin award, which was made to individuals for outstanding contributions to an area of SECT (Office of Science and Technology, 2003), the WISE campaign, and MentorSET, a mentoring scheme developed by the Women's Engineering Society and the Association for Women in Science and Engineering. It provided input and funding to the Portia project, set up by a group of high-level female professionals and centred on a website intended to provide information and support for girls and for women SECT professionals. Other sponsors of Portia included the Post Office, the Institute of Physics, Imperial College London, British Telecom and the Sector Skills Council for Science, Engineering, and Manufacturing Technologies (The Portia Project, 2003).

Although located within the Department of Trade and Industry, the Promoting SET for Women engaged in activities in the educational arena, driven mainly by the received wisdom that gender stereotyping was discouraging girls from taking science and technology subjects. The *Go For It!* poster campaign for schools challenged the masculine image of science with posters showing six young female scientists. Although evaluation suggested that demand for them was enormous, they did not change pupils' attitudes (Promoting SET for Women Unit, 2001, p21). The unit also collaborated with the WISE Campaign and the Engineering Careers Information Service to produce *SPARK* magazine, a bi-annual publication aimed at 11-14 year-old girls, which emphasised the emotional and creative aspects of SECT jobs (Promoting SET for Women Unit, 2001, p23). A video for teachers was produced, entitled *Getting Girls Into Science*, which offered advice about making science more girl friendly (Promoting SET for Women Unit, 2000).

The Unit maintained a strong focus on the women in SECT professions who returned to work. In 2002 it commissioned a study from consultants People Science and Policy Ltd and the Institute for Employment Research at Warwick University, to quantify the number of potential returners and investigate how they could be drawn back into science, engineering and technology jobs. The report mobilised an economic discourse about ensuring a return on state investment in education and training by finding ways to attract potential returners back to work. The authors claimed to have located a pool of economically inactive but qualified women who faced significant barriers when they tried to return to work after extended career breaks and suggested that the government should develop schemes to help them (People Science and Policy Ltd and Institute for Employment Research, 2002). In 2003 the Secretary of State for Trade and Industry, Patricia Hewitt, announced the launch of a new pilot phase of the Teaching Company Scheme aimed specifically at returners who were qualified in science, engineering and technology. Under this scheme companies housed recent graduates working on specific projects and one of its major aims was to convince employers of the business case for gender equality (Promoting SET for Women Unit, 2003).

Women academics were one of the key client groups of the Promoting SET for Women Unit and a major focus of *The Rising Tide* (Committee on Women in Science, Engineering and Technology, 1994). The unit had a major role in funding and setting up the Athena Project, launched in 1999 to promote women's participation and advancement in higher education and research and to achieve better representation of women in top posts (see Chapter Four). The UK higher education funding councils and UniversitiesUK acted as co-sponsors and the project was housed and supported by the Royal Society. Other support came from BP, the Institute of Physics, the European Social Fund, Pfizer, the Royal Academy of Engineering, the Royal Society of Chemistry, and The Wellcome Trust (Royal Society, 2006). Between 1999 and 2001 Athena backed good practice initiatives in twelve higher education institutions, set up five local academic women's networks and produced sixteen good practice guides around topics such as mentoring and networking, career progression and changing SECT cultures (Royal Society, 2006). In the early 2000s Athena became part of the government's Equality Challenge Unit and set up the African-Caribbean Representation in Science and Technology project which focused on the differences between groups of women and men in scientific careers (Bebbington, 2002, p370). Between 2002 and 2004 28 universities piloted Athena's good practice checklist and seven were recognised by the Royal Society Athena Awards. In 2003 the project carried out a series of large-scale surveys of science academics to develop benchmarking tools and to inform policy (Royal Society, 2006).

In 2000 a European Technology Assessment Network (ETAN) group was set up by Nicole Dewandre, head of the Women and Science Unit at the Research Directorate-General of the European Commission. This consisted of senior women scientists and social scientists, was chaired by Professor Mary Osborn and included Teresa Rees and Anne McLaren as UK representatives. The ETAN report, entitled *Science Policies in the European Union: Promoting Excellence Through Mainstreaming Gender Equality,* presented a statistical review of the position of women in higher education, research, industry, and important scientific bodies (Osborn *et al,* 2000). It drew on the business case for gender equality in SECT, bringing the discourse of gender mainstreaming to bear on the issue (Rees, 2001). Its main recommendation was that gender equality should be mainstreamed into European science policy, funding and employment practices (Rees, 2001). Mainstreaming had only been taken up sporadically in the UK and future government intervention in women's participation in SECT would draw more prominently on the corporate discourse of diversity.

In 2001 Sussex University academics Jane Millar and Nick Jagger published a report on a study commissioned by the Department of Trade and Industry, the Department for Education and Employment and the Women's Unit which charted the decline in women's participation in information technology, electronics, and communications (ITEC) and compared it this with the situation in the US, Canada, Ireland, Taiwan, and Spain (Millar and Jagger, 2001). This made use of the business case for women's equality and positioned gender equality within a picture of an information society in which technology would facilitate economic growth, communication and social inclusion. It found that the proportion of women ITEC graduates was lower in the UK than in the other five countries studied. Recommendations included creating multiple points of access to ITEC literacy, tackling the masculine culture of ITEC professions, creating opportunities for career migration and facilitating women's progression within ITEC careers through building confidence and providing opportunities for flexible working (Millar and Jagger, 2001).

Soon after this report appeared, the Equalitec project was set up. This was a partnership of employers, professional bodies and other organisations sponsored by the European Social Fund and the Department of Trade and Industry. The lead partner was the Portia project and others included the British Computer Society, Unilever, Fujitsu, the University of Bath and the Royal Academy of Engineering (Equalitec, 2005). The aim of Equalitec was to develop projects to promote women's participation in ITEC which included a job-based training placement scheme, mentoring circles, training opportunities, a careers portal and an ITEC Innovation Award for outstanding women (Equalitec, 2005). In 2002 a Women in IT conference was held in Whitehall at which the Secretary of State for Trade and Industry spoke. Shortly afterwards the government announced plans for a £1 million recruitment initiative to attract more women into computing jobs by making money available to companies to provide flexible working initiatives (BBC, 2002).

b. The UK Resource Centre for Women in SET
Despite this proliferation of state-sponsored activity, the *Roberts Review* identified a number of serious continuing problems with the supply of science, engineering and technology skills in the UK and highlighted in particular the shortage of women who chose to study these subjects at A-level and in higher education (Roberts, 2002). By the early 2000s the construction industry was having serious recruitment problems with its traditional source of labour, young men aged sixteen to nineteen: attempts to deal with this by enlisting women workers had failed (Gurjao, 2006, p1). In this context Baroness Susan Greenfield submitted the report *SET Fair* to the Office of Science and Technology: this stated that the continued under-representation of women in science, engineering and technology threatened the UK's economic competitiveness and argued that promoting gender equality would provide a return on the investment made in women's training and bring significant economic benefits (Greenfield *et al*, 2002). It recommended that a Working Science Centre be created to support industry and women's groups, that there should be further funding for women returners and

high flyers, that employers should provide greater support with part-time working and job-sharing, that there should be a stronger diversity agenda within national research and development policy and that women should have more input into science policy. It called for more qualitative and quantitative research on women's participation in science, engineering and technology (Greenfield *et al*, 2002).

In response to the Greenfield report the government published a Strategy for Women in Science, Engineering and Technology (Office of Science and Technology, 2003). This pledged to ensure that all government departments were good employers, to improve statistical monitoring, and to set up an independent implementation group of experts from industry and academia to track the progress of the strategy (Office of Science and Technology, 2003). It also agreed to create a UK Resource Centre for Women in SET (UKRC) to take over from the diminishing Promoting SET for Women Unit, whose outgoing Head Pat Langford's brief had shifted to general diversity within the science workforce (personal communication). The UKRC was launched in 2004, sponsored by the Department for Trade and Industry and led by a partnership of Bradford College, Sheffield Hallam University, the Open University and Cambridge University. Its brief was to work with British business to promote the participation of women in SECT, close the skills gap and enhance the country's economic competitiveness (Department of Trade and Industry, 2006b). Within this brief the main objective was to provide advice and support to business about developing best practice (Office of Science and Technology, 2003).

The UKRC was envisaged as an information centre for industry, academia, professional institutes, education and Research Councils within the SECT professions and was intended to support women entering, returning to and progressing in SECT careers (UK Resource Centre for Women in SET, 2006b). Its activities included supporting, advising and working with SECT employers and professional bodies, developing a recognition scheme for good SECT employers, sharing good employment practice, maintaining and disseminating statistics, supporting SECT returners, raising the profile of women in SECT, setting up and running an expert database of women SECT professionals, pump priming projects and providing bursaries for speakers, and co-ordinating the work of women's organisations (UK Resource Centre for

Women in SET, 2004). The UKRC was the lead partner in the JIVE (Joint Intervention) project sponsored by the European Social Fund. JIVE involved ten organisations in Great Britain and had partners in Denmark, Finland, France and Germany. JIVE aimed to promote women's equality in engineering, construction, and technology through a range of activities (Andrew, 2005).

The creation of the UKRC could be viewed as an institutional marrying of state and corporate agendas for women in SECT as its main focus was on industry whereas the Greenfield report focused mainly on women in academia. However, the Centre was also underpinned by an explicit politics since Annette Williams, who had founded the feminist Let's TWIST project at Bradford College (see Chapter Five), headed the team who administered it. From the beginning the work of the UKRC incorporated a feminist focus on women's equality and empowerment which had to be merged with state and corporate economic goals. Williams and other UKRC staff brought with them a history of activism in the women and manual trades movement, which possibly sat uneasily with official preoccupations with female SECT professionals. The UKRC approach was to try to move activity away from deficit models focused on changing women and towards a critical engagement with the culture of SECT professions: an approach discussed in both the ETAN and Greenfield reports and which signalled a shift in the dominant paradigm. This positive development appears to have been propelled by the grounding and experience in feminist ideas and politics of Williams and her team.

In the UKRC, the government had created a large official body with a significant budget to work towards gender equality in SECT. However, due in part to conflicting agendas, the Centre faced challenges in building connections and establishing itself as a significant policy presence. Located in Bradford, it was outside mainstream government machinery. This location could have been an exit strategy for central government as the Department of Trade and Industry moved towards a more amorphous approach to diversity and the Department for Education and Skills agenda remained defined by the issue of boys' underachievement. The formation of a government equality body so far from Whitehall was a surprising decision and threatened to impede UKRC efforts to influence mainstream policy and practice.

3. Initiatives within SECT industries

Industrial initiatives for women in SECT emerged in the context of ideas about skills shortages and intensified during the 1990s alongside the growing trend for corporate diversity imported from the United States. The most thoroughly documented initiatives were those put in place by large national and multi-national companies with the financial and other resources required, although small and medium sized enterprises possibly engaged in activities too, but produced and circulated little documentary evidence. From the 1970s there were corporate initiatives such as scholarships and fellowships for women, internship programmes, school and college outreach work, setting up relationships with student and women's organisations, career development schemes, networks, mentoring programmes, family-friendly and flexible working practices and training on diversity-related issues. There was also industry representation at many of the conferences and events and industry sponsorship of many of the initiatives described here.

The emergent information technology, electronics and communications (ITEC) industry was at the forefront of corporate initiatives for women in SECT. In the 1970s projected skills shortages caused the British computer hardware company International Computers Ltd, part of multinational conglomerate Fujitsu, to state that valuable expertise was being lost when women left work to start families. It invited a woman project manager to set up a flexible working initiative – a small unit of home-based, part-time programmers. This unit grew rapidly and expanded into other work in the industry: by 1984 there were three functional groups in the areas of authoring, software support, and development. But further growth of the initiative was inhibited by inadequate childcare and negative attitudes about the professionalism of the units (Women in Technology, 1984, pp115-116). In the 1980s the company ran a small training course for women returners (Women into IT, 1990a).

In 1988 Women into IT was formed by high-profile employers such as Hewlett-Packard and IBM, supported by the Department of Trade and Industry and professional associations such as the British Computer Society. This nationwide campaign encouraged more women to consider careers in the IT industry and to help employers to make good use of those women already available. Its Professional Development Work-

ing Party focused on encouraging employers to give women opportunities for advancement and publicised best practice in women's professional development, highlighting specific examples with case
studies and awards. The initiative incorporated a Career Enhancement
Working Party with an awards scheme which focused on industrial
career development schemes which particularly benefited women
(Women into IT, 1990a). The government's Central Computer and Tele-
communications Agency responded with an initiative to publicise IT
opportunities for women within various government departments and
offered a CV clearing house for women returners (Women into IT,
1990b).

In the chemicals sector the Chemical and Allied Products Industry
Training Board set up a sponsorship scheme in 1979 to assist companies in facilitating the development of women with management
potential. Grants of up to £1500 per candidate were made available to
individual companies who were then responsible for their own employees (Orchard, 1981). In the 1980s ESSO UK, a division of the multi-
national corporation ExxonMobil, ran awareness-raising seminars
about women's career progression in cooperation with the Industrial
Society. In the drive to facilitate the progression of women within the
company ESSO introduced a career break scheme to allow both men
and women to be absent from work for up to five years, overhauled its
policy on sexual harassment, introduced assertiveness training for all
staff and sponsored courses in management and other areas for women
working at ESSO and other companies. The company got involved in
outreach activities in schools and produced publicity materials about
women in the petroleum industry: in 1984 ESSO UK was one of the
sponsors of Women into Science and Engineering year (Bradby, 1988).
By the early 2000s ExxonMobil had an international diversity programme which covered areas such as education and training, recruitment and career development and flexible working (ExxonMobil, 2001).

The MSF, the trades union for skilled and professional workers which
later became Amicus, became a partner of the Association for Women
in Science and Engineering in the 1990s. In 1995 the two organisations
hosted a conference on the glass ceiling in science, engineering and
technology fields and during the government's science, engineering
and technology week in 1998, the MSF hosted a joint conference with

other unions on gender equality. The MSF, the Association of University Teachers, the National Association of Teachers in Further and Higher Education and IPMS, the union for professionals, managers and specialists also launched a Science Alliance charter which highlighted practical steps to promote women's career development. The MSF created a network for women in science, engineering and technology and conducted a survey about the glass ceiling in the engineering and aerospace industries (Association for Women in Science and Engineering, 1998d). In the 2000s Amicus lobbied for the rights of women in manufacturing, technical and skilled trades, with a campaign to end pay discrimination and to gain representation for women within the union's structures. It held regional and national women's conferences which focused on issues such as pensions, bullying and harassment and maternity rights (Amicus, 2006).

In the 1990s a number of large multinational corporations, including pharmaceuticals giants GlaxoWellcome, which later became Glaxo-SmithKline, and Zeneca, which later became AstraZeneca, became involved in the issue of women in SECT. The GlaxoWellcome Women's Network was launched in 1996: its activities included careers seminars, networking with MPs and Executive Board members, workshops on work/life balance, childcare forums and work with managers on collecting equal opportunities data (Association for Women in Science and Engineering, 1998c). The company put in place a childcare scheme plus a range of flexible working options and offered the Springboard career and personal development programme to its women employees. Glaxo sponsored the Association for Women in Science and Engineering and was a member of Opportunity 2000 (Association for Women in Science and Engineering, 1998a) along with Zeneca. Zeneca implemented recruitment and working practices aimed at facilitating the careers of workers with families such as job sharing, flexible hours, and company-approved career breaks with the facility for maintaining skills and a connection with the industry. The company also offered networking, mentoring, and time and stress management training to all employees. Liaison activities were undertaken with schools, as well as a programme of career discussions between female university students and female managers at Zeneca (Association for Women in Science and Engineering, 1998b). By the late 1990s many corporations had implemented similar gender equality policies and practices, including multinationals British Telecom, Ove Arup, Marconi, Shell, Unilever, and Hewlett-Packard (People Science and Policy Ltd, 2002, p55).

By the early 2000s there were reports of crisis-level skills shortages in information technology, electronics and communications throughout Europe (Millar and Jaggar, 2001). Intellect, the trade association for the UK hi-tech industry, set up a Women in IT forum to promote the participation of women in the industry, increase their representation in senior positions, provide networking and support and to disseminate best practice. The forum sought to promote dialogue around gender equality in the workplace through the engagement of employers and employees. Trade associations, trades unions, government agencies, companies from the IT sector and other sectors with an IT workforce, voluntary sector groups and networking groups all participated in the forum. The Department of Trade and Industry provided support and funding and one of the main functions of the forum was to advise ministers on what initiatives were needed to improve the participation of women in IT and related industries. The forum operated via quarterly meetings featuring topics such as best practice for gender equality, legislation updates and issues around retaining the female workforce. The DTI also sponsored an ongoing research programme on best practice for gender equality, retention, work-life balance and flexible working. There were plans for developing a new initiative to encourage women into IT and to retain existing female workers which specifically addressed issues of workplace culture and difficulties for women returners (Intellect, 2007).

Case study 6.1: Pfizer
Pfizer, an international pharmaceuticals company with various sites in the US and UK, supported the Association for Women in Science and Engineering from its inception in 1994 and was the first corporation to support the Daphne Jackson Trust for women returners, becoming a partner in 2001. The company was also a member of Opportunity Now. In the early 2000s it began to implement its own gender equality initiatives at its Research and Development division at Sandwich in Kent, under the leadership of Trish Lawrence and within its broader diversity strategy. The Research and Development Division employed approxi-

mately 3,600 staff at this time (Pfizer Limited, 2005). Initiatives for women were undertaken with a specific goal to increase the representation of women in key middle and senior management roles and the main policies for achieving this were diversity awareness training, skills-based training, networking and mentoring, flexible working and monitoring and accountability (personal communication).

One of the primary elements of Pfizer's diversity strategy was to make diversity awareness training mandatory for all its managers and supervisors and to build diversity awareness into everyday management practices and appraisals. The company's training package for managers stressed the importance of the business case for promoting diversity and encouraged them to develop an awareness of their own perceptions and the assumptions and stereotypes upon which their judgements about others were based. Progress on fostering diversity was monitored: all managers were expected to improve their ability in the recruitment, development and retention of colleagues from increasingly diverse backgrounds and were appraised accordingly. The company instigated flexible working practices in the early 2000s which included phased return to work after maternity leave and creating a culture within the company which did not discriminate against people working shorter hours. A workplace nursery with 148 places was opened in 2005 and the company planned to offer a returners' package for employees who were returning from a career break: in practice these were mainly women. Under this scheme the manager and the returner would be encouraged to work together, with support to ease the transition back to work (Incomes Data Services, 2006, pp17-20)

The Pfizer Women's Network pre-dated these formal diversity initiatives, and as well as supporting women in the company it engaged in outreach to girls and women in schools and universities to encourage them to take up science and to apply for jobs in industry. The company's Carer's Support Network also supported employees who had caring responsibilities, most of whom were women. As part of Pfizer's overall diversity strategy all its networks were encouraged to set goals, were given a budget and were expected to work with recruitment to widen the talent pool. A web-based mentoring scheme was introduced in 2004 for all employees, with specific mentor-mentee matching and training provided by the company (Incomes Data Services, 2006, p20;

personal communication). In the mid-2000s the company launched two Senior Women's Forums where senior women shared their career trajectories. They identified opportunities and practices that had been helpful, discussed the barriers they had encountered and made specific recommendations for women's advancement within the company. As a result of these forums the company began to review its processes of reward, recognition, and career development for staff and to examine the take-up of its flexible working arrangements. Two similar forums were held for intermediate level women. The company also sponsored the science section of the Confederation of British Industry First Women Awards which recognised women in business who had broken new ground, challenged barriers and prejudices or had opened up opportunities for others to follow (personal communication).

4. Discussion

National government and corporate initiatives to promote the participation of women in SECT happened in the context of globalisation and in a climate in which the state had begun to focus more strongly on women's workforce participation, perhaps aided by increasing numbers of femocrats in senior positions and intensified engagement with the state on the part of feminist groups (Eisenstein, 1991 and 1996; Walby, 2002, pp545-546). However, the overriding factor was the business case for promoting women's participation in SECT or the perceived economic need for their skills, recognised by both government and industry. The business case was mobilised by femocrats and women's groups as part of their political strategies, and the merging of economics and gender equality reached its climax in 2004 with the creation of the UK Resource Centre for Women in SET, a state body run by feminists and with a brief to work closely with employers to increase the representation of women in SECT.

The liberal feminist approaches that, historically, underpinned activity around the issue of women's participation in SECT see the state as a neutral arbiter, mediating between different groups and interests (Blackmore, 1993; Waylen, 1998). However, the involvement of state agencies under Conservative and New Labour administrations was driven by an overtly capitalist agenda. This was symbolised by the key input of the Department of Trade and Industry and for a time personified by Patricia Hewitt, who simultaneously filled the roles of Secretary of State for Trade and Industry and Minister for Women during the early part of New Labour's second term in office. The capitalist agenda for women's equality was further institutionalised in 2003 when the Women and Equality Unit was moved into the Department of Trade and Industry. The DTI took responsibility for the new single equality body, the Commission for Equality and Human Rights which in 2007 subsumed the Equal Opportunities Commission, the Disability Rights Commission and the Commission for Racial Equality (Arnot and Miles, 2005, p184). Thus initiatives for women in SECT were part of a broader trend in which gender equality became part of the neoliberal landscape, often packaged in apolitical and instrumental ways.

Critical and radical feminisms view the state as an institution which has generally acted to reinforce women's subordination throughout history, and as male dominated and which can be theorised as patriarchal (Waylen, 1998; Yeatman, 1993; Randall, 1998; Connell, 1990). The administrative cultures in which bureaucrats work have been identified with the values of the heterosexual, white, technical and rational male and the broader context of hyper-competitive economic globalisation has been theorised as similarly masculine (Blackmore, 1993; Acker, 2004). From this perspective questions arise about the suitability of the state as an agent of gender equality, despite the good intentions of individuals working within it. This casts doubt on the likelihood of success of bodies such as the Promoting SET for Women Unit and the UK Resource Centre for Women in SET. However, the state is not a monolithic entity but a collection of sites, ideologies, people, and processes in which struggles occur and in which interests are actively constructed (Waylen, 1998). The political commitments of individual femocrats and the team running the UKRC have subsisted within the state and could provide a foundation of sympathetic interests for feminist initiatives in the future.

The UKRC provides an example of a collective of feminists and allies working strategically with industry and within the state in the service of gender equality. This can be seen as part of the trend identified by feminist scholars in the 1990s and early 2000s, wherein the women's movement moved from a position of challenging state structures to a stance of accommodation which even built in some aspects of neoliberal ideologies and practices (Banaszak, Beckwith and Rucht, 2003). This model echoes the women's committees within local government which were set up in the 1970s and 80s. Unlike these groups however, the UKRC was set up with a multi-million pound budget and access to a national arena of policy and debate. If femocrats are individual bureaucrats working within state structures, a whole agency run on feminist lines could be a new style of femocratic working (Randall, 1998; Chappell, 2002). The direction UKRC activity takes in the future will show whether this could allow room to work towards a transformative politics of gender.

The possibilities for transformation are limited by the fact that the business case framework within which state and corporate initiatives have been positioned is an inadequate tool for creating change. This rationale for promoting women's participation in SECT does not incorporate an analysis of the causes of gender inequality, so can only inform initiatives at a superficial level. The shift in the early 2000s towards a critical engagement with industry and research cultures was a positive one but initiatives around cultural change can obscure structural inequalities such as pay discrimination, horizontal and vertical labour market segregation, and the gendered divide between public and private life (Wrench, 2005, p80). It is useful to draw on Nancy Fraser's (2001) distinction between the politics of recognition and redistribution, where recognition implies equal respect for different cultures, perspectives and practices and redistribution refers to a more socially just allocation of resources and goods. Initiatives focused on cultural change in SECT can be identified with the principle of recognition which, Fraser argues, has historically proved difficult to combine with a politics of redistribution. Recognition politics may have originated in the arguments of social movements such as feminism and multiculturalism, but the moral elements characterising these have been replaced in the discourse of corporate diversity by neoliberal ideas around business benefits and efficiency (Blackmore, 2006). Within both the business case and diversity frameworks equal opportunities policies are only important as long as there are good business reasons for their existence (Wrench, 2005, pp77-78). There is little room to discuss the exclusion of certain groups as a social injustice, the disadvantages attached to certain categories such as gender, or indeed, the idea of equality as an end in itself (Wrench, 2005, pp80-81).

This illustrates how state and corporate initiatives developed in the interests of global capital may not be in the long term interests of women, even though the goals may temporarily interlock (Volman *et al*, 1995; Henry, 2001). Another potential danger is that market demands could change. This happened when the economic rationalism that encouraged women into SECT during the First and Second World Wars yielded to traditional domestic and gender ideologies after 1945 and most women were displaced to make way for veterans (Kleinman, 1998, p839-840). The business case for women's participation in SECT positions the interests of employers and the interests of women as one and the same but there is a strong possibility that this is not the case. In reporting skills shortages, employers may aim for an over-supply of skilled labour to bid down wages, a not uncommon practice in a highly competitive economy (Gleeson and Keep, 2004). Many companies can generate a profit with a relatively low skilled labour force and often have problems predicting their medium-term skills requirements because of uncertainties around technology, exchange rates and changing corporate strategies (Gleeson and Keep, 2004). There is therefore a risk that in the future women's skills may no longer be needed in SECT fields and that they will be redeployed to other sectors of the economy in the absence of a strong political and moral argument for gender equality in SECT.

This chapter has examined over thirty years of state and corporate activity around women's participation in SECT, which has largely been driven by economic priorities which have temporarily tallied with the equality concerns of feminists and women's groups. State and corporate initiatives undoubtedly had some positive results, but structural inequalities such as labour market segregation and the gender pay gap persisted and work was still organised on a masculine model of the worker even in the early 2000s (Acker 2004, p36). In the corporate world, despite the variety of diversity initiatives, only 3 per cent of the UK's FTSE 100 company executive directors and 10 per cent of non-executive directors were female in 2002 (Point and Singh, 2003, p757). Actions taken to provide flexible working arrangements and childcare in SECT workplaces were constructive, but they fell short of the reorganisation of public and private life that would be needed in order to achieve full equality and which only the state and the corporate world would be in a position to deliver. In addition, the marriage between economics and equal opportunities incorporated tensions between instrumentality and social justice. In the business case for women's participation in SECT, equality was necessary only so long as it provided economic benefits, which left little space for the idea of gender equality as an end in itself. For all these reasons, the initiatives based on this framework may ultimately prove to effect little permanent change.

7

Conclusions

This book provides an overview of a range of initiatives around women's participation in SECT over thirty years. Some are projects carried out in schools, further education colleges and universities, others are independent networking and support groups, membership organisations, women-only training schemes, women's groups within scientific institutions, and large-scale state and corporate interventions. No book can give these projects full justice or represent the commitment and hard work of everyone involved. But it offers a useful reference point for those wishing to explore initiatives around women in SECT, and is a permanent record of an important period of activity.

The first initiatives, discussed in Chapter Three, were targeted at girls and young women in mainstream education and operated in two phases: an initial phase beginning in the 1970s and a resurgence in the mid-1990s. They were mainly classroom-based action research projects, curriculum reforms, independent after-school clubs and awareness-raising campaigns and networks for sharing research findings and good practice. Yet despite all this activity and the intervention of the National Curriculum, pupils' subject choices remained gendered into the 2000s. This was partly due to the complex interaction of social, cultural, educational and psychological factors that structured girls' and young women's educational trajectories, but the initiatives themselves are open to criticism. I challenged the predominant model which situated girls as the problem and attempted to alter their perceptions and choices without engaging critically with science and technology. The common contention that the masculine image of science and technology jarred with prevailing stereotypes of femininity did not take into account the structural and cultural masculinities of SECT and the power and depth of the symbolic association between SECT and masculinity. Consequently the co-construction of gender and SECT should be integrated into mainstream curricula, although this would be difficult to implement within the rigid education system that prevails.

Chapter Four examined initiatives targeted at female SECT professionals – membership organisations, informal networking groups, women's groups within professional associations, groups in universities and courses for women returners. These initiatives have a long history, but many were founded after the 1980s, as interest increased, central government became involved and internet technologies spread. Initiatives for women working in SECT were generally based on a liberal-feminist framework concerned with equal access to SECT professions and helping women to survive and thrive in masculine environments. But the 1990s saw a shift towards reforming masculine cultures in the service of gender equality. I discussed the challenges faced by women's groups in SECT in attempting to critique and change sexist institutions and practices, arguing that the focus of activism should be shifted away from helping women to cope with SECT workplaces and towards more ambitious demands for reforming these environments and reshaping the patriarchal organisation of public and private life. Without engagement with the interaction between patriarchy and the professions, the masculinity of SECT will be preserved and increasing the numbers of women within SECT professions will not bring about the hoped-for transformation.

The field of women-only training in manual trades and technician and user level ICT was explored in Chapter Five. Training schemes for women blended the liberal-feminist concern with equal opportunities with more radical elements of consciousness raising, assertiveness training, validating women's experience and existing knowledge and striving to reform SECT cultures. Courses largely targeted at socially excluded women who had difficulty in accessing mainstream education: fees were waived and free travel and childcare offered in the attempt to overcome structural barriers to women's participation. Such women-only training projects reported successes in both trainees' personal development and their progression into further training and employment. However, many became casualties of shifting funding regimes and the backlash against feminism which gathered pace during the 1990s. The dominant focus of many projects on empowerment for individual women meant that they fostered personal rather than political change, so blunting their radicalism. The goal was empowerment of women through their appropriation of masculine skills but it would have been useful to also challenge the equivalence between technical and craft skills and masculinity so the women trainees could take ownership of their learning.

Chapter Six described state and corporate initiatives around women in SECT which emerged mainly in the mid-1990s alongside an intensified focus on the business case for gender equality and the economic benefits of women's participation in SECT fields. The alliance between economic concerns and women's issues reached its zenith in the formation of the UK Resource Centre for Women in SET, a governmental body with a brief to work with employers to achieve gender equality and cultural change in SECT industries. This was unique in its creation of a feminist organisation within central government that had a significant budget and the potential to influence policy. However, it is dangerous to conceptualise either the state or the market as agents of gender equality, because of the patriarchal character of the state and its historical role in gender-based oppression, plus the market's concern with profit maximisation. The business case framework favoured by state and corporate bodies is an inadequate basis for working towards gender equality: this rationale for women's participation in SECT does not incorporate an explanation of their under-representation nor a framework for the development of initiatives and positions gender equality as instrumental to economic concerns. The language of corporate diversity tends to focus on recognising difference without engaging with how it creates inequality.

Although the initiatives discussed in this book are diverse, they share common themes. Models have mainly been compensatory, focused on either changing girls' and women's perceptions of SECT or giving them the skills and support they need to survive and achieve in SECT fields. This approach works at the level of the individual rather than the social

147

structure and targets girls' and women's internal states, whether attempting to change them or to validate and empower them (Henwood, 1996 and 1998). SECT cultures came under increasing criticism, but this was about recognising gender differences rather than examining gender as a relation of unequal power manifested in the masculinities of SECT environments. Little overt attention was paid to ideas about the co-construction of gender and SECT within the overarching systems of patriarchy and capitalism. Women only training projects and humanistic approaches to teaching science were underpinned by deeper theoretical analyses but to embed such ideas within the activist community of the 2000s demands greater cross-fertilisation with the feminist scholars engaged in deconstructing the relationships between gender and SECT. Such cross-fertilisation has been hindered by the fear that female SECT professionals will be seen as radical, and by the divide between sciences and social sciences in the academy and the growing divergence of academia, activism and educational practice (Phipps, 2006). This book, written by an academic social scientist and targeted at activists, policy-makers and educational practitioners, is an attempt to foster dialogue.

Feminist scholars argue that to understand the causes of women's under-representation in SECT it is necessary to conceptualise SECT and gender as socially produced in interaction with each other and in a patriarchal context. This means trying to theorise the links between structures, cultures, symbols, and gender identities (Wacjman, 2004, pp46, 53; Faulkner, 2001, p82). Gender must be seen as not only a social difference but also as a relation of unequal power. Men's dominance of SECT is the result of horizontal and vertical labour market segregation which positions them as a numerical majority and concentrates them in roles of power and leadership. Horizontal segregation channels men into SECT sectors while women are sorted into occupations such as teaching, healthcare and services. Within a capitalist patriarchy, male-dominated professions often grant money, power and social status. Vertical segregation means that men dominate management and decision making positions in both SECT fields and those which are traditionally female-dominated. This enables men to control women's activities in the workplace and set agendas, define working practices and shape workplace cultures. Labour market segregation is also at the root of the gender pay gap: in 2006, over thirty years after the Equal Pay Act, women working full time still received on average only 87.4 per cent of men's hourly pay (Women and Equality Unit, 2006).

Masculine cultures in SECT have evolved from men's structural dominance and have become so embedded that more than a critical mass of female workers would be needed to reshape them. Women working in SECT must assimilate to these cultures and often rely on supplementary support groups to survive. SECT cultures encompass institutional working practices and individual and group behaviours and are characterised by long working hours, requirement to travel, little support for workers with caring responsibilities, competitive and individualistic values, sexism and sexual harassment, and social activities which do not appeal to female colleagues. These cultures are informed by the symbolic masculinity of SECT and the construction of gender identities within it. Dominant forms of masculinity are associated with certain concepts and ways of behaving entailing rationality, competitiveness, independence, physical strength and technical skill. Such masculinities are central to the definition of the ideal SECT worker because men have historically shaped SECT in the context of a patriarchal social system. This attracts boys and men to SECT at the same time as it drives many girls and women away. The process is circular: the association of SECT and masculinity is both an effect and a cause of men's structural dominance.

The interaction between the structural, cultural and symbolic gendering of SECT is self-perpetuating: men's structural dominance propagates the cultural masculinity of SECT environments and the symbolic association of SECT and masculinity, both of which deter women from participating and reinforce men's structural dominance. But the social nature of this process creates possibilities for intervention. If gender and SECT are both socially shaped then both can be transformed (Faulkner, 2001, p80). Designing an initiative which tackles this complex interaction of factors would be difficult. Macro-level strategies could, however, be worked out among the activist community, arranged around a common set of objectives. The debate would need to engage with the structural, cultural and symbolic, and to tackle recruitment, retention and advancement, as these are often dealt with as separate concerns because of the practicalities of developing and delivering individual projects.

New models should lobby government and mainstream academic and industrial establishments for a major transformation of education and public and private life, since supplementary initiatives too often failed to address fundamental problems and the impression persists that it is the responsibility of women, rather than of the state and the corporate world, to deal with the problem of gender inequality in SECT. Instead of changing women to fit SECT, activities should focus on reshaping SECT to be more welcoming to women from all social backgrounds and to men who do not fit the masculine ideal of the SECT worker.

To end by returning to the beginning of the book, most of the initiatives discussed here operated under multiple constraints. Inadequate funding hindered sustainability, the rigidity of the mainstream curriculum made it difficult to design radical educational projects, feminism and social justice activism suffered a backlash, and challenging SECT from the inside was extremely difficult. Certain initiatives were developed in a neoliberal economic and political context in which equality came second to efficiency and in which inequalities widened between social groups. Given this scenario it is impressive that initiatives around women in SECT have reported any success at all, and I do not wish to detract from this accomplishment. The brief overview presented here is intended to be a catalyst for further research and debate and I hope it will make a modest but valuable contribution to future initiatives around women's participation in SECT.

Bibliography

Acker, J. (2004) 'Gender, Capitalism and Globalization', in *Critical Sociology* 30(1), 17-41

Adam, D. (2005) 'New Royal Society Snub for Greenfield' *The Guardian*, London

Aim Higher (2006) *Aspire AimHigher Southeast London – Women into Construction Fair*. Available online at http://www.aspire-aimhigher.ac.uk/content/view/472/30/

Amicus (2006) *Amicus the Union*. Available online at http://www.amicustheunion.org/

Anderson, J. and Connolly, S. (2006) *Equal Measures: Investigating University Science Pay and Opportunities for Success (research briefing)*. Bradford: UK Resource Centre for Women in SET

Andrew, A. (2005) *JIVE Partners Final Evaluation Report*. Bradford: UK Resource Centre for Women in SET

Apple, M. (2001) 'Comparing Neo-Liberal Projects and Inequality in Education', in *Comparative Education* 37(4), 409-423

Arnot, M. (2002) *Reproducing Gender? Essays on educational theory and feminist politics*. London: Routledge

Arnot, M. and Miles, P. (2005) 'A reconstruction of the gender agenda: the contradictory gender dimensions in New Labour's educational and economic policy', in *Oxford Review of Education* 31(1), 173-189

Arnot, M., David, M. and Weiner, G. (1999) *Closing the Gender Gap: Postwar Education and Social Change*. Cambridge: Polity Press

Aschauer, A. B. (1999) 'Tinkering with Technological Skill: An Examination of the Gendered Uses of Technologies', in *Computers and Composition* 16(1), 7-23

Association for Women in Science and Engineering (1998a) 'GlaxoWellcome', in *Forum* 3 (housed at the UK Resource Centre for Women in SET archive)

Association for Women in Science and Engineering (1998b) 'Zeneca: Providing Equal Opportunities, Nurturing Diversity', in *Forum* 4 (housed at the UK Resource Centre for Women in SET archive)

Association for Women in Science and Engineering (1998c) 'AWISE at GlaxoWellcome', in *Forum* 2 (housed at the UK Resource Centre for Women in SET archive)

Association for Women in Science and Engineering (1998d) 'Women in Science, Engineering, and Technology', in *Forum* 2 (housed at the UK Resource Centre for Women in SET archive)

Association for Women in Science and Engineering (2001a) 'ResNet 2000', in *Forum* 11 (housed at the UK Resource Centre for Women in SET archive)

Association for Women in Science and Engineering (2001b) 'WIN in Pharmaceuticals by Diversity', in *Forum* 11 (housed at the UK Resource Centre for Women in SET archive)

Association of Women in Science and Engineering (2001c) 'National Association of Women Pharmacists', in *Forum* 12 (housed at the UK Resource Centre for Women in SET archive)

Association for Women in Science and Engineering (AWiSE) (2004) *AWiSE website.* Available online at http://www.awise.org/

Athena Project (2005) *UK Assets: 6,500-plus UK scientists can't be wrong* (the Athena surveys). Norwich: University of East Anglia

Atkin, J. M. and Black, P. (2003) *Inside Science Education Reform: a history of curricular and policy change.* Buckingham: Open University Press

BAE Systems (2007) *BAE Systems Education Programme.* Available online at http://www.baesystemseducationprogramme.com/

Bagilhole, B. and Goode, J. (2001) 'The Contradiction of the Myth of Individual Merit, and the Reality of a Patriarchal Support System in Academic Careers: A Feminist Investigation', in *European Journal of Women's Studies* 8(2), 161-180

Ball, S. J. and Vincent, C. (2005) 'The 'childcare champion'? New Labour, social justice, and the childcare market', in *British Educational Research Journal* 31(5), 557-570

Banaszak, L. A., Beckwith, K. and Rucht, D. (2003) 'When Power Relocates: interactive changes in women's movements and states', in L. A. Banaszak, K. Beckwith and D. Rucht (eds) *Women's Movements Facing the Reconfigured State*, 1-29. Cambridge: Cambridge University Press

Bashevkin, S. (2000) 'From Tough Times to Better Times: Feminism, Public Policy, and New Labour Politics in Britain', in *International Political Science Review* 21(4), 407-424

Bassnett, S. (1986) *Feminist Experiences: the Women's Movement in Four Cultures.* London: Allen and Unwin

BCS Women (2007) *BCS Women – home page.* Available online at http://www.bcs.org.uk/bcswomen/

Bebbington, D. (2002) 'Women in Science, Engineering and Technology: a review of the issues', in *Higher Education Quarterly* 56(4), 360-375

Beck, U. and Beck-Gernsheim, E. (2002) *Individualization: Institutionalized Individualism and its Social and Political Consequences.* London: Sage Publications

Bell, J. (2001) 'Patterns of Subject Uptake and Examination Entry 1984-1997', in *Educational Studies* 27(2), 201-219

Benn, R. (1998) 'Still struggling', in R. Benn, J. Elliott and P. Whaley (eds) *Educating Rita and her Sisters: Women and continuing education*, 38-47. Leicester: NIACE

Benn, R., Elliott, J. and Whaley, P. (1998) 'Women and Continuing Education: where are we now?', in R. Benn, J. Elliott and P. Whaley (eds) *Educating Rita and her Sisters: Women and continuing education*, 1-5. Leicester: NIACE

Bennett, J. F., Davidson, M. J. and Gale, A. W. (1999) 'Women in Construction: a comparative investigation into the expectations and experiences of female and male construction undergraduates and employees', in *Women in Management Review* 14(7), 273-291

Benston, M. L. (1992) 'Women's Voices/Men's Voices: technology as language', in G. Kirkup and L. S. Keller (eds) *Inventing Women: Science, Technology and Gender*, 33-41. Cambridge: Polity Press

Bird, E. (2002) 'The Academic Arm of the Women's Liberation Movement: Women's Studies 1969-1999 in the United Kingdom', in *Women's Studies International Forum* 25(1), 139-149

Blackmore, J. (1993) ''In the Shadow of Men': the historical construction of educational administration as a 'masculinist' enterprise', in J. Blackmore and J. Kenway (eds) *Gender Matters in Educational Administration and Policy*, 27-48. London: Falmer Press

Blackmore, J. (1999) 'Localization/globalization and the midwife state: strategic dilemmas for state feminism in education?', in *Journal of Education Policy* 14(1), 33-54

Blackmore, J. (2006) 'Deconstructing Diversity Discourses in the Field of Educational Management and Leadership', in *Educational Management Administration and Leadership* 34(2), 181-199

Blackwell, L. (1992) *Women in the Building Trades: Training and Employment.* London: Women's Education in Building

Blunt, R. (2000) 'Equal to the task? The role of the NUT in promoting equal opportunities in schools', in K. Myers (ed) *Whatever Happened to Equal Opportunities in Schools? Gender Equality Initiatives in Education*, 61-72. Buckingham: Open University Press

Bown, L. (1999) 'Beyond the Degree: men and women at the decision-making levels in British Higher Education', in *Gender and Education* 11(1), 5-25

Bradby, S. (1988) 'Opportunities for Action by Employers' *Women and New Technologies in Training and Employment (seminar proceedings)*, Post House, Edinburgh (housed at the UK Resource Centre for Women in SET archive)

Bradley, H. (1999) *Gender and Power in the Workplace: Analysing the Impact of Economic Change.* Basingstoke: MacMillan Press Ltd

Breakwell, G. M. (1986) 'Young Women on Science and the New Technologies', in J. Harding (ed) *Perspectives on Gender and Science*, 29-39. Lewes: Falmer Press

Breakwell, G. M. and Weinberger, B. (1983) *The Right Women for the Job: recruiting women engineering technician trainees.* London: Manpower Services Commission (housed at the UK Resource Centre for Women in SET archive)

Bridgwood, A. (1991) *Women in Science and Technology: Strategies for Practitioners.* London: Polytechnic of North London (housed at the UK Resource Centre for Women in SET archive)

British Association (1994) *GETSET Programme.* London: British Association and ESSO (housed at the UK Resource Centre for Women in SET archive)

British Broadcasting Corporation (2002) *£1m fund to attract women to tech.* Available online at http://news.bbc.co.uk/1/hi/sci/tech/1765709.stm

British Computer Society (2007) *British Computer Society website.* Available online at http://www.bcs.org.uk/

Brown, A. and Phillips, K. (2000) *Strategic Evaluation of the Information Society Initiative, 1996-2000.* London: DTI Assessment Unit

Brown, C. (1989) 'Girls, boys and technology; getting to the roots of the problem: a study of differential achievement in the early years', in *School Science Review* 71 (255), 138-141

Brown, C. (2001) 'Can Legislation Reduce Gender Differences in Subject Choice? A Survey of GCSE and A level Entries Between 1970 and 1995', in *Educational Studies* 27(2), 173-186

Brown, J. (2005) ''Violent girls': Same or different from 'other' girls?', in G. Lloyd (ed) *Problem girls: understanding and supporting troubled and troublesome girls and young women,* 63-75. Abingdon: RoutledgeFalmer

Bruley, S. (1999) *Women in Britain Since 1900.* Basingstoke: Palgrave

Buckler, S. and Dolowitz, D. P. (2004) 'Can Fair be Efficient? New Labour, Social Liberalism and British Economic Policy', in *New Political Economy* 9(1), 23-38

Bullen, E., Kenway, J. and Hey, V. (2000) 'New Labour, Social Exclusion, and Educational Risk Management: the case of 'gymslip mums'', in *British Educational Research Journal* 26(4), 441-456

Business in the Community (1989) *Women's Enterprise and Training: a briefing paper on women's economic development.* London: Business in the Community (housed at the UK Resource Centre for Women in SET archive)

Business in the Community (2006) *BITC – Opportunity Now.* Available at http://www.bitc.org.uk/programmes/programme_directory/opportunity_now/index.html

Byrne, D. and Madge, B. (1986) 'Women in Physics', in *Physics Bulletin of the Institute of Physics* 37, 454-455 (housed at the UK Resource Centre for Women in SET archive)

Byrne, E. M. (1993) *Women and Science: the snark syndrome.* London: Falmer Press

Cabinet Office (1984) *New Directions in Education and Training for Girls and Women (conference report).* London: HMSO (housed at the UK Resource Centre for Women in SET archive)

Callaghan, J. (2002) 'Social Democracy and Globalisation: the limits of social democracy in historical perspective', in *British Journal of Politics and International Relations* 4(3), 429-451

Callaghan, M., Cranmer, C., Rowan, M., Siann, G. and Wilson, F. (1999) 'Feminism in Scotland: self-identification and stereotypes', in *Gender and Education* 11(2), 161-177

Cambridge AWiSE (2007) *Cambridge AWiSE website.* Available online at http://www.camawise.org.uk/index.html

Carter, R. and Kirkup, G. (1991) 'Redressing the balance: women into science and engineering', in *Open Learning* February 1991, 56-58

Castells, M. (2000) 'The Global Economy', in D. Held and A. Thompson (eds) *The Global Transformations Reader*, 259-273. Cambridge: Polity Press

Central Advisory Council for Education (England) (1959) *A report of the Central Advisory Council for Education (England), Crowther Report.* London: HMSO

Central Advisory Committee for Education (1963) *Half Our Future: Report of the Minister of Education's Central Advisory Council (Newsom Report).* London: Department of Education and Science

Cerny, P. G. and Evans, M. (2004) 'Globalisation and Public Policy Under New Labour', in *Policy Studies* 25(1), 51-65

Change the Face of Construction (2007) *Change the Face of Construction website.* Available online at http://www.change-construction.org/

Chappell, L. (2002) 'The 'Femocrat' Strategy: expanding the repertoire of feminist activists', in *Parliamentary Affairs* 55, 85-98

Chicks with Bricks (2007) *Chicks with Bricks website.* Available online at http://www.chickswithbricks.com/

Clarke, L. and Wall, C. (2004) 'Now you're in, now you're out: women's changing participation in the building trades in Britain', in L. Clarke, E. Michielsens, E. F. Pedersen and B. S. C. Wall (eds) *Women in Construction*, Brussels: European Institute for Construction Labour Research

Clarke, L., Pedersen, E. F., Michielsens, E. and Susman, B. (2005) 'The European Construction Social Partners: Gender Equality in Theory and Practice', in *European Journal of Industrial Relations* 11(2), 151-177

Coats, M. (1994) *Women's Education.* Buckingham: Society for Research into Higher Education and Open University Press

Coats, M. (1996) *Recognising Good Practice in Women's Education and Training.* Leicester: NIACE

Cockburn, C. (1983) *Brothers: Male Dominance and Technological Change.* London: Pluto Press

Cockburn, C. (1985) *Machinery of Dominance: Women, Men, and Technical Know-How.* London: Pluto Press

Cockcroft, W. H. (1982) *Mathematics Counts (The Cockcroft Report).* London: HMSO

Committee on the Public Understanding of Science (2004) *COPUS Grant Schemes.* Available online at http://www.copus.org.uk/

Committee on Women in Science, Engineering, and Technology (1994) *The Rising Tide: a report on women in science, engineering and technology.* London: HMSO

Connell, R. W. (1990) 'The state, gender, and sexual politics: theory and appraisal', in *Theory and Society* 19(5), 507-544

Connell, R. W. and Wood, J. (2005) 'Globalization and Business Masculinities', in *Men and Masculinities* 7(4), 347-364

Construction Industry Training Board (2006) *Construction Industry Training Board website.* Available online at http://www.citb-constructionskills.co.uk

Cook, L. and Martin, J. (2005) *35 Years of Social Change.* Manchester: Equal Opportunities Commission

Craig, J. and Harding, J. (1985) *Girls and Science and Technology: the third international GASAT conference report.* London: King's College London (housed at the UK Resource Centre for Women in SET archive)

Cullity, J. and Younger, P. (2004) 'Sex Appeal and Cultural Liberty: A Feminist Inquiry into MTV India', in *Frontiers* 25(2), 96-122

Dainty, A. R. J., Bagilhole, B. M. and Neale, R. H. (2001) 'Male and female perspectives on equality measures for the UK construction sector', in *Women in Management Review* 16(6), 297-304

Dale, R., Bowe, R., Harris, D., Loveys, M., Moore, R., Shilling, C., Sikes, P., Trevitt, J. and Valsecchi, V. (1990) *The TVEI Story: Policy, practice and preparation for the workforce.* Milton Keynes: Open University Press

Daly, M. (2005) 'Gender Mainstreaming in Theory and Practice', in *Social Politics: International Studies in Gender, State and Society* 12(3), 433-450

Daphne Jackson (1985) *Fellowships for Women Returners to Science and Engineering: report on the appointment of the first group of fellows* (housed at the UK Resource Centre for Women in SET archive)

Daphne Jackson Trust (2007) *Welcome to the Daphne Jackson Trust.* Available online at http://www.daphnejackson.org/

Dawe, J. and Rhydderch, G. (1983) 'The Tameside Girls and Science Initiative' *Contributions to the Second GASAT conference*, 233-245. Oslo: University of Oslo (housed at the UK Resource Centre for Women in SET archive)

Department for Communities and Local Government (2006) *Department for Communities and Local Government website.* Available online at http://www.communities.gov.uk

Department for Education and Employment (2000) Labour Market and Skill Trends 2000. Nottingham: DfEE Publications

Department for Education and Skills (2005) *14-19 Education and Skills.* London: HMSO

Department of Education and Science (1975) *Curricular Differences for Boys and Girls: education survey 21*. London: HMSO (housed at the UK Resource Centre for Women in SET archive)

Department of Education and Science (1978) *Girls and Science (matters for discussion 13)*. London: HMSO (housed at the UK Resource Centre for Women in SET archive)

Department of Trade and Industry (1999) *Women and Information and Communication Technologies: a literature review*. London: Department of Trade and Industry

Department of Trade and Industry (2006a) *Construction Statistics Annual Report*, 2006. London: HMSO

Department of Trade and Industry (2006b) *DTI website*. Available online at http://www.dti.gov.uk

Department of Trade and Industry and Opportunity 2000 (1995) *Making the Most: Women in Science, Engineering, and Technology*. London: HMSO

Devins, D., Darlow, A. and Smith, V. (2002) 'Lifelong Learning and Digital Exclusion: Lessons from the Evaluation of an ICT Learning Centre and an Emerging Research Agenda', in *Regional Studies* 36(8), 941-945

Dietz, M. G. (2003) 'Current Controversies in Feminist Theory', in *Annual Review of Political Science* 6, 399-431

Digital Womens Network (2006) *Digital Womens Network – Home*. Available online at http://www.digitalwomensnetwork.org/

DigitalEve (2007) *DigitalEve website*. Available online at http://www.digitaleve.org/index.html

Division for the Advancement of Women (United Nations) (2006a) *Commission on the Status of Women*. Available online at http://www.un.org/womenwatch/daw/csw/index.html

Division for the Advancement of Women (United Nations) (2006b) *Convention on the Elimination of All Forms of Discrimination Against Women*. Available online at http://www.un.org/womenwatch/daw/cedaw/index.html

Dobrowolsky, A. (2002) 'Crossing Boundaries: Exploring and Mapping Women's Constitutional Interventions in England, Scotland and Northern Ireland', in *Social Politics: International Studies in Gender, State and Society* 9, 293-340

Doherty, M. (1987) 'Science Education for Girls: a case study', in *School Science Review* 69(246), 28-33

Eatwell, R. (2003) 'The Currents of Political Thought', in J. Hollowell (ed) *Britain Since 1945*, 161-178. Oxford: Blackwell

Eclipse Publications (1990) *Equal Opportunities Review 30*. London: Eclipse Publications (housed at the UK Resource Centre for Women in SET archive)

Eisenstein, H. (1991) *Gender Shock: Practicing Feminism on Two Continents*. Boston: Beacon Press

Eisenstein, H. (1996) *Inside Agitators: Australian Femocrats and the State*. Philadelphia: Temple University Press

Eisenstein, H. (2005) 'A Dangerous Liaison? Feminism and Corporate Globalization', in *Science and Society* 69(3), 487-518

Ellen, D. and Herman, C (2005) *Training and Employment of Women ICT Technicians: a report of the JIVE MCSE Project*. Buckingham: Open University

Ellis, J. (1986) *Equal Opportunities and Computer Education in the Primary School*. Manchester: Equal Opportunities Commission (housed at the UK Resource Centre for Women in SET archive)

Ellis, P. (2003) 'Women in Science-Based Employment: What Makes the Difference?', in *Bulletin of Science, Technology and Society* 23(1), 10-16

Ellison, N. and Ellison, S. (2006) 'Creating 'Opportunity for All'? New Labour, New Localism, and the Opportunity Society', in *Social Policy and Society* 5(3), 337-348

Engineering Industry Training Board (1987) *Women in Engineering: EITB Initiatives*. Watford: Engineering Industry Training Board (housed at the UK Resource Centre for Women in SET archive)

Equal Opportunities Commission (1985) *Girls and Information Technology: report of a project in the London Borough of Croydon to evaluate guidelines for good practice in the IT curriculum*. Manchester: Equal Opportunities Commission (housed at the UK Resource Centre for Women in SET archive)

Equal Opportunities Commission (2000) *Women and Men in Britain: at the millennium*. Manchester: Equal Opportunities Commission

Equal Opportunities Commission (2001) *Sex Stereotyping: from school to work*. Manchester: Equal Opportunities Commission

Equal Opportunities Commission (2002) *Evidence to the House of Commons Science and Technology Committee Inquiry: Science Education 14-19*. Manchester: Equal Opportunities Commission

Equal Opportunities Commission (2004) *Facts About Women and Men in Britain 2004*. Manchester: Equal Opportunities Commission

Equal Opportunities Commission (2006) *EOC website*. Available online at http://www.eoc.org.uk

Equal Opportunities Commission (2007) *What is the Gender Equality Duty?* Available online at http://www.eoc.org.uk/Default.aspx?page=17686

Equal Opportunities Commission and Engineering Council (1984) *Calendar of Events Planned for Women into Science and Engineering Year*. London: Equal Opportunities Commission and Engineering Council (housed at the UK Resource Centre for Women in SET archive)

Equalitec (2005) *Equalitec Advancing Women*. Available online at http://www.equalitec.org.uk

Eschle, C. (2002) 'Engendering Global Democracy', in *International Feminist Journal of Politics* 4(3), 315-341 e-skills UK (2006) *CC4G: Computer Clubs for Girls (introductory leaflet)*. London: e-skills UK

e-skills UK (2007) *e-skills website*. Available online at http://www.e-skills.com/

Esslemont Group (2007) *Esslemont Group, University of Aberdeen*. Available online at http://www.abdn.ac.uk/esslemontgroup/

European Social Fund (2003) 'Building up the construction industry – Overview', in *ESF News Magazine* 11((Dec 2003)).

Evaluation Associates Ltd (1995) *COPUS: The Committee on the Public Understanding of Science: an evaluation of schemes and projects*. Buckingham: Evaluation Associates Ltd (housed at the UK Resource Centre for Women in SET archive)

ExxonMobil (2001) *Global Diversity 2001*. London: ExxonMobil

Faludi, S. (1992) *Backlash: the undeclared war against women*. London: Chatto and Windus

Farnsworth, K. (2006) 'Capital to the Rescue? New Labour's business solutions to old welfare problems', in *Critical Social Policy* 26(4), 817-842

Faulkner, W. (2001) 'The Technology Question in Feminism: a view from feminist technology studies', in *Women's Studies International Forum* 24(1), 79-95

Faulkner, W. (2002) *Women, gender in/and ICT: Evidence and reflections from the UK (SIGIS report)*. Edinburgh: University of Edinburgh

Faulkner, W. (2004) *Strategies of Inclusion: Gender and the Information Society (final report of the SIGIS project)*. Edinburgh: University of Edinburgh

Faulkner, W. and Kleif, T. (2003) *Edinburgh Women's Training Course: an old idea still working*. Edinburgh: University of Edinburgh

Featherstone, B. (2006) 'Rethinking Family Support in the Current Policy Context', in *British Journal of Social Work* 36, 5-19

Ferry, G. (1985) 'Was WISE Worthwhile?' in *The New Scientist* (housed at the UK Resource Centre for Women in SET archive)

Flory, L. (2004) *Understanding Eating Distress*. London: MIND (National Association for Mental Health)

Fox Keller, E. (1985) *Reflections on Gender and Science*. New Haven, Connecticut: Yale University Press

Fox Keller, E. F. (1992) 'How Gender Matters, or why it's so hard for us to count past two', in G. Kirkup and L. S. Keller (eds) *Inventing Women: Science, Technology and Gender,* 42-56. Cambridge: Polity Press

Francis, B. (1999) 'Lads, Lasses and (New) Labour: 14-16-year-old students' responses to the 'laddish behaviour and boys' underachievement' debate', in *British Journal of Sociology of Education* 20(3), 355-371

Francis, B. (2000) 'The Gendered Subject: students' subject preferences and discussions of gender and subject ability', in *Oxford Review of Education* 26(1), 35-48

Fraser, N. (1997) *Justice Interruptus*. London: Routledge

Fraser, N. (2001) 'Recognition Without Ethics?', in *Theory, Culture and Society* 18(2-3), 21-42

Further Education Unit (1981) *Balancing the Equation: a study of women and science and technology within FE.* London: HMSO (housed at the UK Resource Centre for Women in SET archive)

Further Education Unit (1985) *Changing the Focus: Women and FE.* London: Further Education Unit (housed at the UK Resource Centre for Women in SET archive)

General NVQ (1996) *Promoting Women into Technology GNVQs: project report.* London: General NVQ (housed at the UK Resource Centre for Women in SET archive)

Genz, S. (2006) 'Third Way/ve: the politics of postfeminism', in *Feminist Theory* 7(3), 333-353

Gibbs, S. and Thompson, D. L (1992) 'Huddersfield WIT', in *Physics Education* 27, 254-257

Gilbert, J. (2001) 'Science and its 'Other': looking underneath 'woman' and 'science' for new directions in research on gender and science education', in *Gender and Education* 13(3), 291-305

Gillborn, D. and Mirza, H. S. (2000) *Educational inequality: mapping race, class, and gender.* London: Office for Standards in Education

Girls into Science and Technology (1979) *Girls into Science and Technology Introductory Booklet.* Manchester: Manchester Polytechnic (housed at the UK Resource Centre for Women in SET archive)

Girls into Science and Technology (1984) *Girls into Science and Technology Final Report.* Manchester: Manchester University (housed at the UK Resource Centre for Women in SET archive)

Gleeson, D. and Keep, E. (2004) 'Voice without accountability: the changing relationship between employers, the State and education in England', in *Oxford Review of Education* 30(1), 37-63

Grant, L. (2006) *CREST Awards Evaluation: impact study.* Liverpool: Liverpool University

Greenfield, S., Peters, J., Lane, N., Rees, T. and Samuels, G. (2002) *SET Fair: A Report on Women in Science, Engineering and Technology, from The Baroness Greenfield CBE to the Secretary of State for Trade and Industry.* London/Norwich: HMSO

Griffin, G. (2003) 'Constitutive Subjectivities: Contemporary Black and Asian Women Playwrights in Britain', in *The European Journal of Women's Studies* 10(4), 377-394

Griffiths, D. (1985) 'The exclusion of women from technology', in W. Faulkner and E. Arnold (eds) *Smothered by Invention: technology in women's lives*, 51-71. London: Pluto Press

Grosser, K. and Moon, J. (2005) 'The Role of Corporate Social Responsibility in Gender Mainstreaming', in *International Feminist Journal of Politics* 7(2), 532-554

Gurjao, S. (2006) *Inclusivity: the Changing Role of Women in the Construction Workforce.* London: Chartered Institute of Building

Hall, R. and Sandler, B. (1982) *The Classroom Climate: a chilly one for women.* Washington DC: Association of American Colleges (housed at the UK Resource Centre for Women in SET archive)

Harding, J. (1975) 'What action should we take?', in Centre for Science Education (ed) *Girls and Science Education: cause for concern?*, 74-79 (housed at the UK Resource Centre for Women in SET archive)

Harding, J. and Craig, J. (1978) *Girls and Science Education Project (internal report).* London: Chelsea College (housed at the UK Resource Centre for Women in SET archive)

Harding, J. and Randall, G. (1983) 'Why Classroom Interaction Studies?' *Contributions to the Second GASAT conference*, 41-52. Oslo: University of Oslo (housed at the UK Resource Centre for Women in SET archive)

Harding, S. (1986) *The Science Question in Feminism.* Milton Keynes: Open University Press

Harding, S. (1992) 'How the Women's Movement Benefirs Science: two views', in G. Kirkup and L. S. Keller (eds) *Inventing Women: Science, Technology and Gender*, 57-72. Cambridge: Polity Press

Harding, S. and Hintikka, M. B. (1983) 'Introduction', in S. Harding and. M. B. Hintikka (eds) *Discovering Reality: Feminist Perspectives on Epistemology, Metaphysics, Methodology, and Philosophy of Science*, London: D. Reidel Publishing Company

Harris, A. (2004) *Future Girl: Young Women in the Twenty-First Century.* London: Routledge

Hatfield, D. (2005) *The Women's Engineering Society: a little bit of history.* Presented at the 2005 WES conference, available online at http://www.wes.org.uk/online publications.shtml

Hawkesworth, M. (1999) 'Analyzing Backlash: Feminist Standpoint Theory as an Analytical Tool', in *Women's Studies International Forum* 22(2), 135-155

Haywoode, T. L. (1983) college for Neighbourhood Women: Innovation and Growth, in Charlotte Bunch and Sandra Pollack (eds) *Learning Our Way: Essays in Feminist Education.* New York: The Crossing Press

Head, J. (1983) 'Sex Differences in Adolescent Personality Development and the Implications for Science Education' *Contributions to the Second GASAT conference*, 53-61. Oslo: University of Oslo (housed at the UK Resource Centre for Women in SET archive)

Hearn, M. (1979) 'Girls for physical science: a school based strategy for encouraging girls to opt for the physical sciences', in *Education in Science* 82, 14-16

Henry, M. (2001) 'Globalisation and the Politics of Accountability: issues and dilemmas for gender equity in education', in *Gender and Education* 13(1), 87-100

Henwood, F. (1996) 'WISE Choices? Understanding Occupational Decision-making in a Climate of Equal Opportunities for Women in Science and Technology', in *Gender and Education* 8(2), 199-214

Henwood, F. (1998) 'Engineering Difference: discourses on gender, sexuality and work in a college of technology', in *Gender and Education* 10(1), 35-49

Henwood, F. (2000) 'From the Woman Question in Technology to the Technology Question in Feminism: Rethinking Gender Equality in IT Education', in *European Journal of Women's Studies* 7(2), 209-227

Henwood, F. and Miller, K. (2001) 'Boxed in or Coming out? On the Treatment of Science, Technology and Gender in Educational Research', in *Gender and Education* 13(3), 237-242

Her Majesty's Inspectorate (1991) *Technical and Vocational Education Initiative (TVEI), England and Wales 1983-90*. London: HMSO

HighTech Women (2004) *HiTech Women website*. Available online at http://www.hightech-women.com/

Hildebrand, G. (1989) 'Gender Inclusive Science Education: the work of the McClintock Collective' *Gender and Science and Technology: contributions to the 5th international conference (volume 1)*, 87-95. Haifa: Israel Institute of Technology (housed at the UK Resource Centre for Women in SET archive)

Hindmoor, A. (2005) 'Public Policy: Targets and Choice', in *Parliamentary Affairs* 58(2), 272-285

Hipperson, S. (2006) *Greenham Common Women's Peace Camp, 1981-2000*. Available online at http://www.greenhamwpc.org.uk/

Holton, V. (1989) *The Female Resource: an overview*. Berkhamsted: Ashridge Management Research Group (housed at the UK Resource Centre for Women in SET archive)

Hughes, G. (2001) 'Exploring the Availability of Student Scientist Identities within Curriculum Discourse: an anti-essentialist approach to gender-inclusive science', in *Gender and Education* 13(3), 275-290

Incomes Data Services (2006) 'Plugging the Talent Pipeline at Pfizer', in *Diversity at Work* 22, 17-20

Inner London Education Authority (1975) *Careers Opportunities for Women and Girls*. London: Inner London Education Authority (housed at the UK Resource Centre for Women in SET archive)

Institute of Employment Studies (1995) *Balancing the Building Team: Gender Issues in the Building Professions*. Brighton: Institute for Employment Studies

Institute of Physics (2006a) *Girls in the Physics Classroom: a teachers' guide for action*. London: Institute of Physics

Institute of Physics (2006b) *Women in University Physics Departments: a site visit scheme 2003-2005*. London: Institute of Physics

Institute of Physics (2007) *Institute of Physics – home of the Institute of Physics.* Available online at http://www.iop.org/

Intellect (2007) *Intellect website.* Available online at http://www.intellectuk.org/default. asp

Jacks, H. (1988) 'Women Caught Sleepering on the Job' *Press and Journal* (housed at the UK Resource Centre for Women in SET archive)

Jacob, K. and Licona, A. C. (2005) 'Writing the Waves: A Dialogue on the Tools, Tactics, and Tensions of Feminisms and Feminist Practices Over Time and Place', in *National Women's Studies Association Journal* 17(1), 197-205

JIVE (2006) *JIVE home page.* Available online at http://www.jivepartners.org.uk/index. htm

Jones, S. (2004) 'Women Doctors at Top 'harm status' *The Guardian*, London.

Julius, D. (2000) *New Trends in a New Economy?* Annual Prestige Lecture: Chartered Institute of Bankers

Keep, E. (2005) 'Reflections on the curious absence of employers, labour market incentives and labour market regulation in English 14-19 policy: first signs of a change in direction?', in *Journal of Education Policy* 20(5), 533-553

Kelly, A. (1975) 'A discouraging process: how girls are eased out of science', in Centre for Science Education (ed) *Girls and Science Education: cause for concern?*, 1-18 (housed at the UK Resource Centre for Women in SET archive)

Kelly, A. (1987) 'Introduction', in A. Kelly (ed) *Science for Girls?*, NEED PAGES. Milton Keynes: Open University Press

Kelly, A. (1988) *Getting the GIST: A Quantitative Study of the Effects of the Girls into Science and Technology Project (Manchester Sociology Occasional Papers).* Manchester: University of Manchester (housed at the UK Resource Centre for Women in SET archive)

Kleif, T. and Faulkner, W. (2003) *'I am not the same person!' User Study of a Women-Only Training Course.* Edinburgh: University of Edinburgh

Kleinman, S. S. (1998) 'Overview of Feminist Perspectives on the Ideology of Science', in *Journal of Research in Science Teaching* 35(8), 837-844

Lee, D. (1996) *TVEI and Curriculum Theory.* Humberside: David Lee and Humberside Education Services

Leicester City Council (2006) *Leicester City Council – Women in Construction.* Available online at http://www.leicester.gov.uk/index.asp?pgid=28182

Let's TWIST (2001) *Let's TWIST Newsletter: Issue 1.* Bradford: Bradford College

Let's TWIST (2004) *Let's TWIST.* Available online at http://letstwist.bradfordcollege. ac.uk

Lewis, J. (1992) *Women in Britain Since 1945.* Oxford: Basil Blackwell Ltd.

Lewis, J. (2003) 'Women and Social Change 1945-1995', in J. Hollowell (ed) *Britain Since 1945*, 260-278. Oxford: Blackwell

Lie, S. (1983) *Girls and Science and Technology: the second international GASAT conference report.* Oslo: University of Oslo (housed at the UK Resource Centre for Women in SET archive)

Lister, R. (2002) 'The dilemmas of pendulum politics: balancing paid work, care and citizenship', in *Economy and Society* 31(4), 520-532

Loader, B. D. and Keeble, L. (2004) *Challenging the Digital Divide: a literature review of community informatics initiatives.* York: Joseph Rowntree Foundation

London Development Agency (2001) *£4.4 million boost for skills in London.* Available online at http://www.lda.gov.uk

Madden, A. (2000) 'An episode in the thirty years war: race, sex, and class in the ILEA 1981-90', in K. Myers (ed) *Whatever Happened to Equal Opportunities in Schools? Gender Equality Initiatives in Education*, 27-60. Buckingham: Open University Press

Magalhâes, A. M. and Stoer, S. R. (2003) 'Performance, Citizenship and the Knowledge Society: a new mandate for European education policy', in *Globalisation, Societies and Education* 1(1), 41-66

Manpower Services Commission (1988) *Report on Young Women in YTS Conference and Competition.* London: Manpower Services Commission (housed at the UK Resource Centre for Women in SET archive)

Mansbridge, J. (2003) 'Anti-statism and Difference Feminism in International Social Movements', in *International Feminist Journal of Politics* 5(3), 355-360

Manthorpe, C. (1987) 'Reflections on the Scientific Education of Girls', in *School Science Review* March 1987, 422-431

Marshall, C. (1997) 'Undomesticated Gender Policy', in B. J. Bank and P. M. Hall (eds) *Gender Equity and Schooling: Policy and Practice*, pp63-91. New York: Garland Publishing Inc

Mason, G. (1999) *The Labour Market in Science and Engineering Graduates: are there Mismatches between Supply and Demand? Department for Education and Employment, Research Brief No. 112.* London: HMSO

McGivney, V. (1998) 'Dancing into the future: developments in adult education', in R. Benn, J. Elliott and P. Whaley (eds) *Educating Rita and her Sisters: Women and continuing education*, 9-17. Leicester: NIACE

McGuigan, J. (2003) 'Cultural Change', in J. Hollowell (ed) *Britain Since 1945*, 279-295. Oxford: Blackwell

MentorSET (2006) *MentorSET Home.* Available online at http://www.mentorset.org.uk/

Meredith, S. (2006) 'Mr Crosland's Nightmare? New Labour and Equality in Historical Perspective', in *British Journal of Politics and International Relations* 8, 238-255

Millar, J. and Jaggar, N. (2001) *Women in ITEC Courses and Careers.* Nottingham: Department for Education and Skills Publications

Mitter, S. (1995) 'Who Benefits? Measuring the Differential Impact of New Technologies', in Gender Working Group, United Nations Commission on Science and

Technology for Development (ed) *Missing Links: Gender Equity in Science and Technology for Development*, 219-242. Ottawa: International Development Research Centre

Morton, S. and Price, J. (1984) *Girls' Education in Mathematics, Science, and Technology: Interim Project Report.* Nottingham: Nottinghamshire County Council (housed at the UK Resource Centre for Women in SET archive)

Mums in Science (2007) *Mums in Science website.* Available online at http://www.mumsinscience.net

Murphy, P. and Whitelegg, E. (2006) *Girls in the Physics Classroom: A Review of the Research on the Participation of Girls in Physics.* London: Institute of Physics

Myers, K. (2000) 'How Did We Get Here?', in K. Myers (ed) *Whatever Happened to Equal Opportunities in Schools? Gender Equality Initiatives in Education*, 1-9. Buckingham: Open University Press

Nash, K. (2002) 'A Movement Moves... Is There a Women's Movement in England Today?', in *European Journal of Women's Studies* 9(3), 311-328

National Association of Women in Construction (2007) *National Association of Women in Construction website.* Available online at http://www.nawic.co.uk/

National Association of Women Pharmacists (2003) *NAWP – National Association of Women Pharmacists.* Available online at http://www.nawp.org.uk/

National Electronics Council (Undated) *Girls in Electronics and IT.* London: National Electronics Council (housed at the UK Resource Centre for Women in SET archive)

National Statistics (2006) *Internet Access: houses and individuals (first release).* London: HMSO

NISUS Scotland (2003) *Edinburgh Women's Training Course.* Available online at http://www.ewtc.co.uk/

North Devon College (2006) *Employers: Women into Construction.* Available online at http://www.ndevon.ac.uk/information/13/construction/wom_into_const.htm:

Oakley, A. (1974) *The Sociology of Housework.* London: Martin Robertson

Office of Science and Technology (1993) *Realising Our Potential: A Strategy for Science, Engineering and Technology.* London: HMSO

Office of Science and Technology (1994) *Women in Science, Engineering and Technology: Government Response to the Report, The Rising Tide: Women in Science, Engineering and Technology.* London: HMSO

Office of Science and Technology (2003) *A strategy for women in science, engineering, and technology.* London: HMSO

O'Hara, G. and Parr, H. (2006) 'Conclusions: Harold Wilson's 1964-70 Governments and the Heritage of New Labour', in *Contemporary British History* 20(3), 477-489

Oliver, K. L. and Lalik, R. (2001) 'The body as curriculum: learning with adolescent girls', in *Journal of Curriculum Studies* 33(3), 303-333

Open University (2006) *Science, Engineering, and Technology: a course for women returners.* Available online at http://www3.open.ac.uk/courses/bin/p12.dll?C02T160. Buckingham: Open University

Open University Women into Science and Engineering Group (1991) *WISE Research Group Workshop Report on Teaching Electronics to Women.* Milton Keynes: Open University (housed at the UK Resource Centre for Women in SET archive)

Opportunity 2000 (1996) *Tapping the Talent.* Available at http://info.lboro.ac.uk/orgs/opp2000/:

Orchard, L. (1981) 'The Chemical and Allied Products ITB Sponsorship Scheme for Women', in C. L. Cooper (ed) *Practical Approaches to Women's Career Development,* St Hugh's College, Oxford. (housed at the UK Resource Centre for Women in SET archive)

Orr, P. (2000) 'Prudence and progress: national policy for equal opportunities (gender) in schools since 1975', in K. Myers (ed) *Whatever Happened to Equal Opportunities in Schools? Gender Equality Initiatives in Education,* 13-26. Buckingham: Open University Press

Osborn, M., Rees, T., Bosch, M., Ebeling, H., Hermann, C., Hilden, J., McLaren, A., Palomba, R., Peltonen, L., Vela, C., Weis, D., Wold, A., Mason, J. and Wennerås, C. (2000) *Science Policies in the European Union: Promoting excellence through mainstreaming gender equality.* Brussels: European Commission

Oxford City Council (2006) *Oxford Women's Training Scheme.* Available online at http://www.oxford.gov.uk/business/oxford-womens-training.cfm

Paechter, C. (1992) 'Gendered Subjects Coming Together: Power and Gender in the Design and Technology Curriculum for England and Wales' *GASAT East and West European conference: contributions (volume 1),* 31-40. Eindhoven: Eindhoven University of Technology (housed at the UK Resource Centre for Women in SET archive)

Parker, L. (2003) 'The Evolving Gender-ICT Agenda in Education' *Keynote address to GASAT 11 conference (from conference proceedings),* Mauritius: Mauritius Institute of Education (housed at the UK Resource Centre for Women in SET archive)

Pascall, G. and Lewis, J. (2004) 'Emerging Gender Regimes and Policies for Gender Equality in a Wider Europe', in *Journal of Social Policy* 33(3), 373-394

Peacock, S. (1983) *The technician in engineering: employment, education and training of women technicians.* London: Engineering Industry Training Board

People Science and Policy Ltd and Institute for Employment Research (2002) *Maximising Returns to Science, Engineering, and Technology Careers.* London: HMSO

Perriton, L. (2007) 'Forgotten Feminists: the Federation of British Professional and Business Women, 1933-1969', in *Women's History Review* 16(1), 79-97.

Perrons, D. (2005) 'Gender Mainstreaming and Gender Equality in the New (Market) Economy: An Analysis of Contradictions', in *Social Politics: International Studies in Gender, State and Society* 12(3), 389-411

Pfizer Limited (2005) *Pfizer website.* Available online at http://www.pfizer.co.uk/

Phipps, A. (2005) 'Women in Science, Engineering, and Technology: Researching the arena of activity', Unpublished PhD thesis: Faculty of Education, University of Cambridge

Phipps, A. (2006) "I can't do with whinging women!' Feminism and the habitus of 'women in science' activists', in *Women's Studies International Forum* 29(6), 125-135

Phipps, A. (2007) 'Re-inscribing Gender Binaries: Deconstructing the dominant discourse around women's equality in science, engineering, and technology', in *The Sociological Review*, 55(4), 768-787

Physics Education Committee (1982) *Girls and Physics*. London: Royal Society and Institute of Physics (housed at the UK Resource Centre for Women in SET archive)

Pilcher, J., Delamont, S., Powell, G. and Rees, T. (1989) 'Challenging Occupational Stereotypes: Women's training roadshows and guidance at school level', in *British Journal of Guidance and Counselling* 17(1), 59-67

Pilcher, J., Delamont, S., Powell, G., Rees, T. and Reed, M. (1989) 'Evaluating a Women's Careers Convention: methods, results, and implications', in *Research Papers in Education* 4(1), 57-76

Pillbeam, S. and Farren, S. (2004) *EVE: Constructing Futures, Engineering Change*. South East Derbyshire College:

Pitt, L. (2003a) *IT Beat: bringing pop and glamour to IT (SIGIS case study)*. Edinburgh: University of Edinburgh

Pitt, L. (2003b) New Media, Old World: the Untold Story (SIGIS case study). Edinburgh: University of Edinburgh

Platt of Writtle, The Baroness (1988) 'Equal Opportunities in Science and Engineering', in *School Science Review* 62(249), 639-647

Point, S. and Singh, V. (2003) 'Defining and Dimensionalising Diversity: Evidence from Corporate Websites Across Europe', in *European Management Journal* 21(6), 750-761

Pope, R. (1998) *The British Economy Since 1914: A Study in Decline?* London: Longman

Portia Project (2003) *Portia – SET for all women*. Available online at http://www.portiaweb.org

Portsmouth Girls' School (1991) *Engineering Club introductory leaflet*. Portsmouth: Portsmouth Girls' School (housed at the UK Resource Centre for Women in SET archive)

Prentice, S. (2000) 'The Conceptual Politics of Chilly Climate Controversies', in *Gender and Education* 12(2), 195-207

Preston, P. and MacKeogh, C. (2003) *Strategies of Inclusion: Gender and the Information Society (case studies of private efforts to include women in ICT)*. Edinburgh: University of Edinburgh

Price, J. and Talbot, B. (1984) 'Girls and Physical Science at Ellis Guilford School', in *School Science Review* 66(234), 7-11

Promoting SET for Women Unit (2000) *Engaging Girls in SET – information bulletin 1*. London: Office of Science and Technology

Promoting SET for Women Unit (2001) *Get With It! Adopting a creative approach to engaging girls in science, engineering, and technology.* London: HMSO

Promoting SET for Women Unit (2003) *SET 4 Women website (archive version).* Available from UK Resource Centre for Women in SET:

Promoting Women in Construction (2006) *Promoting Women in Construction – the Centre for the Built Environment.* Available online at http://www.pwic.co.uk/

Pugh, M. (2000) *Women and the Women's Movement in Britain, Second Edition.* Basingstoke: MacMillan Press

Queen Mary University of London (2006) *News and Events.* Available online at http://www.dcs.qmul.ac.uk/newsevents/detail.php?n=2006-03-06%2012%3A10%3A57

Raat, J. H., Harding, J. and Mottier, I. (1981a) *Girls and Science and Technology conference book 1981. Eindhoven: Eindhoven University of Technology* (housed at the UK Resource Centre for Women in SET archive)

Raat, J. H., Harding, J. and Mottier, I. (1981b) *Proceedings GASAT conference 1981.* Eindhoven: Eindhoven University of Technology (housed at the UK Resource Centre for Women in SET archive)

Ramsden, J. M. (1990) 'All Quiet on the Gender Front?', in *School Science Review* 72(295), 49-55

Randall, V. (1998) 'Gender and power: women engage the state', in Vicky Randall and Georgina Waylen (eds) *Gender, Politics, and the State*, pp185-205. London: Routledge

Reay, D. (2005) 'Beyond Consciousness: the Psychic Landscape of Social Class', in Sociology 39(5), 911-928

Rees, T. (2001) 'Mainstreaming Gender Equality in Science in the European Union: the 'ETAN' Report', in *Gender and Education* 13(3), 243-260

Rees, T. (2005) 'Reflections on the Uneven Development of Gender Mainstreaming in Europe', in *International Feminist Journal of Politics* 7(4), 555-574

ResNET (2007) *ResNET: home.* Available online at http://www.uea.ac.uk/csed/resnet/welcome.htm

Roberts, G. (2002) *SET for success: The supply of people with science, technology, engineering and mathematics skills.* London: HMSO

Rommes, E., Oudshoorn, N. and Stienstra, M. (2003) *KidCom designer case (SIGIS report).* Edinburgh: University of Edinburgh

Rose, H. (1994) *Love, Power and Knowledge: Towards a Feminist Transformation of the Sciences.* Cambridge: Polity Press

Rose, H. (1999) 'A Fair Share of the Research Pie or Re-Engendering Scientific and Technological Europe?', in *European Journal of Women's Studies* 6, 31-47

Rosser, S. (2005) 'Through the Lenses of Feminist Theory: Focus on Women and Information Technology', in *Frontiers* 26(1), 1-23

Rowbotham, S. (1989) *The Past is Before Us: Feminism in Action Since the 1960s.* London: Penguin

Royal Society (2006) *Athena Project website.* Available at http://www.athenaproject. org.uk

Royal Society (2007) *Gender profile of the fellowship.* Available online at http://www. royalsoc.ac.uk/page.asp?id=2214

Royal Society of Chemistry (2007) *Women Members Network.* Available online at http://www.rsc.org/Membership/Networking/WomenMembersNetwork/

Rubery, J. (2005) 'Reflections on Gender Mainstreaming: An Example of Feminist Economics in Action?', in *Feminist Economics* 11(3), 1-26

Rushall, C. (2001) *Carole Rushall.* Available online at http://www.dur.ac.uk/c.a.rushall/

Sampaio, A. (2004) 'Transnational Feminisms in a New Global Matrix', in *International Feminist Journal of Politics* 6(2), 181-206

Saunderson, W. (2002) 'Women, Academia and Identity: Constructions of Equal Opportunities in the 'New Managerialism' – A Case of Lipstick on the Gorilla?', in *Higher Education Quarterly* 56(4), 376-406

Science Policy Support Group (1992a) *Women and Science Newsletter, Issue 2.* London: Economic and Social Research Council (housed at the UK Resource Centre for Women in SET archive)

Science Policy Support Group (1992b) *Women and Science Newsletter, Issue 4.* London: Economic and Social Research Council (housed at the UK Resource Centre for Women in SET archive)

Scottish Executive (2006) *Scottish Childcare.* Available online at https://www.scottish childcare.gov.uk/

Segal, L. (1987) *Is the Future Female? Troubled thoughts on contemporary feminism.* London: Virago Press Ltd

Segal, L. (2000) 'Only Contradictions on Offer', in *Women: a cultural review* 11(1/2), 19-36

Seldon, A. and Collings, D. (2000) *Britain Under Thatcher.* Essex: Pearson Education

Selwyn, N. and Gorard, S. (2003) 'Reality bytes: examining the rhetoric of widening educational participation via ICT', in *British Journal of Educational Technology* 34(2), 169-181

SETNET (2007) *SETNET homepage.* Available online at http://www.setnet.org.uk/

Shaw, E. (2003) 'Britain Left Abandoned? New Labour in Power', in *Parliamentary Affairs* 56, 6-23

Sheffield Hallam University (2006) *West of Scotland Science, Engineering and Technology Returners Project for Women.* Available online at http://extra.shu.ac.uk/ nrc/section_0/events_images/1895%20returners_leaflet.pdf

Sked, A. and Cook, C. (1993) *Post-war Britain: a political history.* Harmondsworth: Penguin

Skelton, C. (1998) 'Feminism and Research into Masculinities and Schooling', in *Gender and Education* 10(2), 217-227

Skills and Enterprise Network (2001) *Labour Market Quarterly Report*. Sheffield: Skills and Enterprise Network

Smith, P. and Morton, G. (2006) 'Nine Years of New Labour: Neoliberalism and Workers' Rights', in *British Journal of Industrial Relations* 44(3), 401-420

South West Women in Construction (2006) *SWWIC South West Women in Construction*. Available online at http://www.swwic.co.uk/index.php

Squires, J. and Wickham-Jones, M. (2004) 'New Labour, Gender Mainstreaming and the Women and Equality Unit', in *British Journal of Politics and International Relations* 6, 81-98

Stanton, W. (2004) 'British Radio Dramaturgy and the Effects of the New Conservatism', in *New Theatre Quarterly* 20(1), 59-68

Stewart, J. (2002) 'Information society, the Internet and gender: a summary of pan-European statistical data', in K. H. Sorensen and J. Stewart (eds) *Digital Divide and Inclusion Measures: A review of Literature and statistical Trends on Gender and ICT*, 1-20. Trondheim: NTNU

Strathdee, R. (2005) 'Globalization, innovation, and the declining significance of qualifications led social and economic change', in *Journal of Education Policy* 20(4), 437-456

Swarbrick, A. and Atkins, R. (1991) 'WIT: ten years of positive action', in *The Woman Engineer* Spring 1991, 7-9

Swarbrick, A., Atkins, R., Harris, J., Johnson, J., Willoughby, L., Ashman, S. and Mirfield, V. (1990) *Women in Technology: Interim Report to the Training Agency*. Buckingham: Open University and Loughborough University of Technology (housed at the UK Resource Centre for Women in SET archive)

Swarbrick, A., Atkins, R., Harris, J., Johnson, J., Ashman, S. and Mirfield, V. (1993) *Women in Technology: Report to the Training Agency*. Buckingham: Open University and Loughborough University of Technology (housed at the UK Resource Centre for Women in SET archive)

Taber, K. S. (1991) 'Girl-friendly physics in the National Curriculum', in *Physics Education* 26(4), 221-226

Taylor, C., Fitz, J. and Gorard, S. (2005) 'Diversity, specialisation, and equity in education', in *Oxford Review of Education* 31(1), 47-69

The Association of Women in Property (2007) *Women in Property website*. Available online at http://www.wip.propertymall.com/

Toller, P. W., Suter, E. A. and Trautman, T. C. (2004) 'Gender Role Identity and Attitudes Towards Feminism', in *Sex Roles* 51(1-2), 85-90

Training Services Agency (1975) *Training Opportunities for Women*. London: Manpower Services Commission (housed at the UK Resource Centre for Women in SET archive)

Tuana, N. (1992) 'The Radical Future of Feminist Empiricism', in *Hypatia: A Journal of Feminist Philosophy* 7(1), 99-113

UK Resource Centre for Women in SET (2004) *SETting the Standard: UK resource centre for women in science, engineering and technology.* Available online at http://extra.shu.ac.uk/nrc/section_0/UKRC%20Strategy%20Guide.pdf

UK Resource Centre for Women in SET (2005a) *Annual Review May 2004 – April 2005.* Bradford: UK Resource Centre for Women in SET

UK Resource Centre for Women in SET (2005b) *Statistics on Women in SET.* Bradford: UK Resource Centre for Women in SET

UK Resource Centre for Women in SET (2006a) *Annual Review, May 2005 – April 2006.* Bradford: UK Resource Centre for Women in SET

UK Resource Centre for Women in SET (2006b) *UKRC website.* Available online at http://www.setwomenresource.org.uk

UK Resource Centre for Women in SET (2007) *Statistics on Women in SET (available on request).* Bradford: UK Resource Centre for Women in SET

University of Cambridge (2006) *WiSETI – the University of Cambridge Women in Science, Engineering, and Technology Initiative.* Available online at http://www.admin.cam.ac.uk/offices/personnel/equality/wiseti/

Vauxhall College of Building and Further Education (1985) *Equal Opportunities Staff Development Programme.* London: Vauxhall College of Building and Further Education (housed at the UK Resource Centre for Women in SET archive)

Vlaeminke, M., McKeon, F. and Comber, C. (1997) *Breaking the Mould: An Assessment of Successful Strategies for Attracting Girls into Science, Engineering and Technology.* London: HMSO (housed at the UK Resource Centre for Women in SET archive)

Vogler, C. (2005) 'Cohabiting Couples: rethinking money in the household at the beginning of the twenty first century', in *The Sociological Review* 53(1), 1-29

Volman, M., van Eck, E. and Ten Dam, G. (1995) 'Girls in Science and Technology: the development of a discourse', in *Gender and Education* 7(3), 283-292

Wai Yin Chinese Women Society (2006) *Women Construction Solutions.* Available online at http://www.waiyin.org.uk/projects/diy/index.html

Wajcman, J. (2000) 'Reflections on Gender and Technology Studies: In What State is the Art?', in *Social Studies of Science* 30(3), 447-464

Wajcman, J. (2004) *Technofeminism.* Cambridge: Polity Press

Walby, S. (1990) *Theorizing Patriarchy.* Oxford: Blackwell

Walby, S. (2002) 'Feminism in a Global Era', in *Economy and Society* 31(4), 533-557

Walford, G. (1980) 'Sex Bias in Physics Textbooks', in *School Science Review* 62(219), 220-227

Walker, H. (2002) *CiWAG – brief history.* Available online at http://www.sstd.rl.ac.uk/rascwiag/history.htm

Walker, H. (2006) *RAS Committee for Women in Astronomy and Geophysics*. Available online at http://www.sstd.rl.ac.uk/rascwiag/default.htm

Walkerdine, V. (1983) 'Some Issues in the Historical Construction of the Scientific Truth About Girls' *Contributions to the Second GASAT conference*, 79-91. Oslo: University of Oslo (housed at the UK Resource Centre for Women in SET archive)

Walkerdine, V. (1988) *The Mastery of Reason: cognitive development and the production of rationality*. London: Routledge

Walkerdine, V. (1998) *Counting Girls Out: Girls and Mathematics (new edition)*. London: Falmer Press

Walton, A. (1984) *It's a Woman's World Too! Science and Engineering*. London: City of London Polytechnic Learning and Library Resources Service (housed at the UK Resource Centre for Women in SET archive)

Warrington, M. and Younger, M. (2000) 'The Other Side of the Gender Gap', in *Gender and Education* 12(4), 493-508

Warrior, J. (1997) *Cracking It! Helping Women to Succeed in Science, Engineering, and Technology*. London: Engineering Council (housed at the UK Resource Centre for Women in SET archive)

Waters, M. (2001) *Globalization (Second Edition),* Second Edition. London: Routledge

Watson, P. (2000) 'Rethinking Transition: Globalism, Gender, and Class', in *International Feminist Journal of Politics* 2(2), 183-213

Waylen, G. (1998) 'Gender, feminism, and the state: an overview', in V. Randall and G. Waylen (eds) *Gender, Politics and the State*, 1-17. London: Routledge

Waylen, G. (2006) 'You still don't understand: why troubled engagements continue between feminists and (critical) IPE', in *Review of International Studies* 32, 145-164

Weiner, G. (1994) *Feminisms in Education: an introduction*. Buckingham: Open University Press

West, A. and Pennell, H. (2002) 'How New is New Labour? The Quasi Market and English Schools 1997 to 2001', in *British Journal of Educational Studies* 50(2), 206-224

Whelehan, I. (2000) *Overloaded: Popular Culture and the Future of Feminism*. London: The Women's Press

Whitelegg, E., Murphy, P., Scanlon, E. and Hodgson, B. (1992) 'Investigating Collaboration in Primary Science Classrooms: a gender perspective' *GASAT East and West European conference: contributions (volume 1)*, 77-90. Eindhoven: Eindhoven University of Technology (housed at the UK Resource Centre for Women in SET archive)

Wilkinson, H. (1999) 'The Thatcher Legacy: Power Feminism and the Birth of Girl Power', in N. Walter (ed) *On the Move: Feminism for a New Generation*, London: Virago Press

Williams, R. (1991) 'Technology in Context' *Action for Equity: the Second Decade (GASAT Six conference contributions, volume 2)*, 798-806. Melbourne: National Key Centre for School Science and Mathematics (housed at the UK Resource Centre for Women in SET archive)

WiSET (2006) *WISET Home Page*. Available online at http://www.eps.manchester.ac.uk/wise/

WITNET (2007) *Women in Technology Network*. Available online at http://www.plymouth.ac.uk/witnet

Witz, A. (1992) *Professions and Patriarchy*. London: Routledge

Women @ CL (2005-2007) *Computer Laboratory – Women @ CL*. Available online at http://www.cl.cam.ac.uk/women/ Cambridge: University of Cambridge

Women and Equality Unit (2004) *Equality, Opportunity, and Choice: Tackling Occupational Segregation*. London: HMSO

Women and Equality Unit (2006) *Women and Equality Unit website*. Available at http://www.womenandequalityunit.gov.uk/

Women and Manual Trades (1978) *Women and Manual Trades Newsletter*. London: Women and Manual Trades (soon to be available online at http://www.wamt.org)

Women and Manual Trades (1980) *Women and Manual Trades Newsletter*. London: Women and Manual Trades (soon to be available online at http://www.wamt.org)

Women and Manual Trades (1981) *Women and Manual Trades Newsletter*. London: Women and Manual Trades (soon to be available online at http://www.wamt.org)

Women and Manual Trades (1983) *Women and Manual Trades Newsletter*. London: Women and Manual Trades (soon to be available online at http://www.wamt.org)

Women and Manual Trades (1984) *Women and Manual Trades Newsletter*, January 1984. London: Women and Manual Trades (soon to be available online at http://www.wamt.org)

Women and Manual Trades (1985) *Women and Manual Trades Newsletter*, Winter 1985. London: Women and Manual Trades (soon to be available online at http://www.wamt.org)

Women and Manual Trades (1987) *Women and Manual Trades Newsletter*, June 1987. London: Women and Manual Trades (soon to be available online at http://www.wamt.org)

Women and Manual Trades (1993) *Women and Manual Trades Newsletter*, Spring 1993. London: Women and Manual Trades (soon to be available online at http://www.wamt.org)

Women and Manual Trades (1995) *Women and Manual Trades Newsletter*, Spring 1995. London: Women and Manual Trades (soon to be available online at http://www.wamt.org)

Women and Manual Trades (2000) *Building the Future: 25 Years of Women and Manual Trades*. London: Women and Manual Trades

Women and Manual Trades (2001) *Women and Manual Trades Newsletter*, Winter 2001. London: Women and Manual Trades (soon to be available online at http://www.wamt.org)

Women and Manual Trades (2002) *Women and Manual Trades Newsletter*, Summer 2002. London: Women and Manual Trades (soon to be available online at http://www.wamt.org)

Women and Manual Trades (2006) *Women and Manual Trades website*. Available online at http://www.wamt.org

Women Connect (1999) *A report on women and Information and Communication Technologies (ICTs) for PAT 15*. London: Women Connect

Women for Science for Women (1987) *Women for Science for Women, Newsletter No 1*. London: Women for Science for Women (housed at the UK Resource Centre for Women in SET archive)

Women in Architecture (2007) *Women in Architecture*. Available online at http://www.diversecity-architects.com/WIA/wia.htm

Women in Construction Advisory Group (1985) *Report on the work of the Women in Construction Advisory Group*. London: Women in Construction Advisory Group (housed at the UK Resource Centre for Women in SET archive)

Women in Construction Alliance (1994) *WICA Newsletter, Issue 1*. London: Women in Construction Alliance (housed at the UK Resource Centre for Women in SET archive)

Women in London (2004) *Women in London: a directory of London-based women's groups*. Available online at http://www.womeninlondon.org.uk

Women in Physics Group (2001) *Women in Physics Group – archived home page*. Available online at http://groups.iop.org/WP/archive

Women in Physics Group (2004) *Women in Physics Group – home page*. Available online at http://groups.iop.org/WP

Women in Plumbing Group (2006) *Women in Plumbing Group – the Institute of Plumbing and Heating Engineering*. Available online at http://www.iphe.org.uk/wip.html

Women in Property (2007) *Women in Property*. Available online at http://www.wipnet.org/

Women in Science, Engineering, and Technology (WiTEC), (2000) *European Database of Women Experts in Science, Engineering, and Technology (conference proceedings)*. London: European Commission, Employment and Social Affairs; Promoting SET for Women Unit

Women in Technology (1984) *Women in Technology: proceedings of a conference held at Loughborough University, January 1984*. Loughborough: Women in Technology (housed at the UK Resource Centre for Women in SET archive)

Women in Telecoms and Technology (2007) *WiTT | Home*. Available online at http://www.wittgroup.org/

Women into Computing (1988) *Women into Computing Conference Proceedings.* London: Women into Computing (housed at the UK Resource Centre for Women in SET archive)

Women into Computing (2007) *Women into Computing website.* Available online at http://www.wic.org.uk/index.htm

Women into IT (1990a) *Women into IT Newsletter Issue 1.* Farnborough: Women into IT (housed at the UK Resource Centre for Women in SET archive)

Women into IT (1990b) *Women into IT Newsletter Issue 2.* Farnborough: Women into IT (housed at the UK Resource Centre for Women in SET archive)

Women into Science and Engineering (1984) *WISE Education and Training Conference: Abstracts of Invited Talks and Conference Proceedings.* London: Women into Science and Engineering (housed at the UK Resource Centre for Women in SET archive)

Women into Science and Engineering (1987) *Women Into Science and Engineering: Progress and Prospects (conference report).* London: Women into Science and Engineering (housed at the UK Resource Centre for Women in SET archive)

Women into Science and Engineering (1988) *Directory of Initiatives 1988.* London: women into Science and Engineering

Women into Science and Engineering (1999) *WISE Vehicle Programme: Technology in Action for Girls.* London: Women into Science and Engineering (housed at the UK Resource Centre for Women in SET archive)

Women into Science and Engineering (2000a) *Engineering Equals: a booklet for staff in primary schools.* London: Engineering and Marine Training Authority

Women into Science and Engineering (2000b) *Engineering Equals: a booklet for staff in secondary and further education.* London: Engineering and Marine Training Authority

Women into Science and Engineering (2001a) *A Girl Like You.* London: Women into Science and Engineering

Women into Science and Engineering (2001b) *Speaking Out: Creativity, People, Teamwork.* London: Women into Science and Engineering

Women into Science and Engineering (WISE) Working Group (1987) *WISE Working Group Report 1984-1987.* Buckingham: Open University (housed at the UK Resource Centre for Women in SET archive)

Women into Science and Engineering Campaign (1988) *Directory of Initiatives 1988.* London: WISE Campaign (housed at the UK Resource Centre for Women in SET archive)

Women into Science and Engineering Campaign (2006a) *Directory of Initiatives 2006.* London: WISE Campaign

Women into Science and Engineering Campaign (2006b) *WISE Campaign website.* Available online at http://www.wisecampaign.org.uk

Womenintechnology (2007) *Womenintechnology website*. Available online at http://www.womenintechnology.co.uk/content_static/home.asp

Women's Education in Building (1994) *The WEB Report: Training women in the construction trades*. London: Women's Education in Building (housed at the UK Resource Centre for Women in SET archive)

Women's Engineering Society (2007) *Women's Engineering Society website*. Available online at http://www.wes.org.uk/

Women's National Commission (1987) *Women's Training Roadshows: how to run them*. London: Cabinet Office (housed at the UK Resource Centre for Women in SET archive)

Women's National Commission (2005) *The Women's National Commission*. Available online at http://www.thewnc.org.uk/index.html

Women's Training Network (Undated) *Women's Training Workshops (promotional leaflet)*. Leeds: Women's Training Network (housed at the UK Resource Centre for Women in SET archive)

Women's Workshop (2006) *Women's Workshop website*. Available online at http://www.womensworkshop.org.uk

Working Group on 14-19 Reform (2004) *14-19 Curriculum and Qualifications Reform*. London: Department for Education and Skills

Wrench, J. (2005) 'Diversity management can be bad for you', in *Race and Class* 46(3), 73-84

Yeatman, A. (1993) 'Contemporary Issues for Feminism: the Politics of the State', in J. Blackmore and J. Kenway (eds) *Gender Matters in Educational Administration and Policy,* 137-145. London: Falmer Press

Yeomans, D. (1996) *Constructing Vocational Education: from TVEI to GNVQ (Occasional Paper No. 1)*. Leeds: 14-19 Research Group, University of Leeds

Young Women's Christian Organisation (2005) *YWCA England and Wales response to the Women and Work Commission's call for evidence*. Oxford: Young Women's Christian Organisation

Young, M. F. D. (1998) *The Curriculum of the Future: From the 'new sociology of education' to a critical theory of learning*. London: Falmer Press

YWCA of Great Britain (1991) *A Report on a Training Course for Young Women in Manual Trades*. Devon: YWCA of Great Britain (housed at the UK Resource Centre for Women in SET archive)

Zukas, M. (1998) 'Locating women, theorising women', in R. Benn, J. Elliott and P. Whaley (eds) *Educating Rita and her Sisters: Women and continuing education*, 28-37. Leicester: NIACE

Index

INDEX

181